Synthesis Lectures on Computer Science

The series publishes short books on general computer science topics that will appeal to advanced students, researchers, and practitioners in a variety of areas within computer science.

Roberto Andrade · Carlos Ayala ·
Paulina Morillo

Building Ethical and Secure AI

Principles, Practices, and Challenges for the Next Generation

Springer

Roberto Andrade
Colegio de Ciencias e Ingenierías
Universidad San Francisco de Quito
Quito, Ecuador

Carlos Ayala
Facultad de Ingeniería de Sistemas
Escuela Politécnica Nacional
Quito, Ecuador

Paulina Morillo
Department of Computer Science
Universidad Politécnica Salesiana
Quito, Ecuador

ISSN 1932-1228 ISSN 1932-1686 (electronic)
Synthesis Lectures on Computer Science
ISBN 978-3-032-25788-8 ISBN 978-3-032-25789-5 (eBook)
https://doi.org/10.1007/978-3-032-25789-5

This Springer imprint is published by the registered company Springer Nature Switzerland AG
The registered company address is: Gewerbestrasse 11, 6330 Cham, Switzerland

We dedicate this book to those who believe that technology should serve humanity, not the other way around; to the students, researchers, and professionals who work tirelessly to build a fairer, more transparent, and responsible artificial intelligence. May these pages be an invitation to think, to question, and to transform the future with ethics and hope.

Preface

The age of Artificial Intelligence is not a speculative future—it is a present reality shaping decisions in health care, employment, finance, and social well-being. As intelligent systems increasingly permeate domains where the stakes are human rights, dignity, and equity, the demand for ethical, transparent, and resilient AI is no longer optional but imperative.

This book address to that challenge by bridging the theoretical foundations of AI ethics with engineering practices and policy considerations, anchored in four representative and high-impact scenarios: **health care allocation**, **pregnancy prediction**, **personnel selection**, and **credit granting**. Each of these exercises illustrates how algorithmic bias, opaque models, and weak governance can amplify existing social inequities and introduce new harms. These domains are not chosen arbitrarily—they are emblematic of what scholars and regulators increasingly refer to as "critical AI deployments" due to the intensity of ethical risk and societal sensitivity they entail.

This book is structured to provide a progressive, interdisciplinary journey across nine chapters, each tackling a foundational dimension required to build *trustworthy AI systems*. The narrative begins with a diagnosis of ethical stakes in high-consequence domains and continues through the evolution of regulatory frameworks, techniques to mitigate algorithmic bias, and the imperative of cybersecurity as a moral duty. The book also explores the dangers of dual-use AI and the risks of malicious deployment, transitioning toward methods for eliciting ethical and legal requirements, the integration of formal guarantees, and systemic approaches to security, resilience, and multi-level governance.

Our goal is to equip AI engineers, policy makers, researchers, and students with a holistic framework for responsible AI development, rooted in real-world tensions and governed by formal rigor.

Quito, Ecuador
August 2025

Roberto Andrade
Carlos Ayala
Paulina Morillo

Acknowledgements

We would like to express our deepest gratitude to all those who contributed to the creation of this book. In particular, we thank Julia Leticia Cabrera, a student of the Computer Science program at Universidad San Francisco de Quito, for her dedicated work in reviewing each chapter, ensuring that the content remained clear, practical, and accessible, and for her valuable input in closing each section with meaningful reflections. We also express our sincere appreciation to Diego Vallejo-Huanga for his insightful contributions to the diverse topics on Artificial Intelligence discussed throughout this work, enriching the depth and scope of our analysis.

Finally, we extend our appreciation to colleagues, mentors, and students whose feedback and perspectives inspired us to refine our ideas, and to our families for their unwavering support throughout this journey. This book is as much a product of collective effort as it is of individual dedication.

Contents

Acronyms

AI	Artificial Intelligence
DoS	Denial of Service
DP	Differential Privacy
EU AI Act	European Union Artificial Intelligence Act
GDPR	General Data Protection Regulation
GORE	Goal-Oriented Requirements Engineering
ISO	International Organization for Standardization
KAOS	Knowledge Acquisition in autOmated Specification
LIME	Local Interpretable Model-Agnostic Explanations
LLM	Large Language Model
ML	Machine Learning
NIST	National Institute of Standards and Technology
OWASP	Open Worldwide Application Security Project
SHAP	SHapley Additive exPlanations
XAI	Explainable Artificial Intelligence

Part I
Building Ethical AI: From Philosophy to Implementation

Artificial Intelligence does not emerge in a vacuum—it is shaped by the values, intentions, and assumptions embedded in its design. Part I explores the foundational ethical and epistemological underpinnings of AI, guiding the reader from abstract philosophical principles to their practical realization in system architecture and engineering workflows. This part begins by tracing the historical evolution of ethical AI, then investigates critical domains where AI exercises consequential decision-making, such as healthcare, criminal justice, and social services. It also addresses the transition from high-level norms—such as fairness, transparency, and inclusivity—to formalized technical specifications and requirements. By integrating ethics-by-design approaches and stakeholder-centered perspectives, Part I builds a framework for translating moral imperatives into computational action.

Critical Domains of AI Deployment: Ethical Stakes and Engineering Challenges 1

1.1 Introduction

This book adopts an approach to applied ethical AI by contextualizing its content through four hands-on exercises aligned with USAID's Ethics AI Guide [1]. This guide developed by the United States Agency for International Development (USAID) proposes the responsible design, deployment, and evaluation of artificial intelligence systems in critical sectors such as healthcare, education, finance, and governance. USAID's Ethics AI Guide emphasizes five core principles that underpin ethical and responsible AI:

1. **Transparency**: AI systems must be understandable, traceable, and auditable. Developers should document data provenance, algorithms used, and provide meaningful explanations of automated decisions.
2. **Fairness**: AI systems should avoid reinforcing historical or social biases. Measures must be taken to mitigate discrimination against marginalized groups based on gender, ethnicity, age, disability, or socioeconomic status.
3. **Privacy and Security**: Sensitive data must be protected with strong cybersecurity and data governance practices. Individuals must retain agency through informed consent and robust safeguards against data misuse.
4. **Sustainability**: AI interventions should be environmentally, socially, and economically sustainable. They must be resilient over time without creating technological dependence.
5. **Inclusivity**: Communities affected by AI systems should participate in their development. Stakeholders must be engaged to ensure cultural relevance and contextual appropriateness.

R. Andrade et al., *Building Ethical and Secure AI*, Synthesis Lectures on Computer Science,
https://doi.org/10.1007/978-3-032-25789-5_1

USAID's Ethical AI guidance analyzes social contexts where AI deployment has produced harmful outcomes, highlighting the need for responsible innovation. In this book, we focus on four specific cases that reflect high-stakes applications: healthcare access prediction, pregnancy risk classification, personnel selection, and credit allocation. These exercises show how ethical imperatives can be translated into actionable engineering practices, offering a pathway toward socially responsible and context-aware AI systems:

1. **Healthcare Access Prediction USAID Context**: This case aligns with USAID's principles of *inclusive development* and the mandate to *do no harm*, especially when deploying AI systems in health-sensitive contexts. In this context, the following ethical stakes are identified:

- **Bias Risk**: Socioeconomic and demographic disparities may cause the model to unfairly deny healthcare access to underrepresented or historically marginalized populations.
- **Privacy**: The use of health-related features involves processing highly sensitive data, requiring rigorous protections to avoid ethical breaches and trust erosion.

2. **Pregnancy Risk Prediction USAID Context**: This exercise aligns with USAID's principles of gender equity, youth empowerment, and healthcare vulnerability mitigation. In this context, the following ethical stakes are identified:

- **Gendered Outcomes**: Predictive models may inadvertently reproduce patriarchal biases if not validated with sensitivity to socio-cultural norms.
- **Agency**: There is a risk of *automated paternalism*, where algorithmic outputs constrain personal decision-making autonomy.

3. **Personnel Selection USAID Context**: This use case corresponds with labor rights, non-discrimination, and the promotion of fair employment practices. In this context, the following ethical stakes are identified:

- **Disparate Impact**: Protected attributes such as gender, age, or ethnicity might introduce hidden barriers to equitable hiring.
- **Transparency & Contestability**: Applicants should be able to understand and contest algorithmic decisions regarding employment.

4. **Credit Allocation Equity USAID Context**: This task supports economic empowerment, financial inclusion, and anti-poverty objectives. In this context, the following ethical stakes are identified:

- **Economic Discrimination**: If fairness constraints are not applied, models may reinforce historical exclusions from credit access.

- **Accountability**: Financial institutions must provide algorithmic explanations for credit denials, upholding institutional trust.

The importance of designing AI solutions based on Ethical AI Frameworks lies in their capacity to align technical development with human-centered values:

- **Protecting Vulnerable Populations**: AI used in development often targets low-resource environments where risks of harm or exclusion are amplified. Without safeguards, these technologies can unintentionally perpetuate injustice or bias.
- **Ensuring Accountability and Trust**: Public sector and donor-funded projects require transparency and explainability to maintain legitimacy. Ethical AI supports auditability and contestability of algorithmic decisions.
- **Preventing Harm**: By embedding a "do-no-harm" mindset, developers can anticipate adverse consequences such as surveillance misuse, exclusion from services, or unintended harms due to automation.
- **Promoting Social Trust and Long-Term Adoption**: Ethical guidelines foster public confidence and encourage the integration of AI into sustainable, locally accepted development strategies.

While we have used the scenarios outlined in the USAID AI Ethics Guidelines as a primary reference, there are other frameworks that also address the ethical challenges of artificial intelligence and incorporate principles similar to the five previously discussed. Table 1.1 presents a synthesis of representative Ethical AI frameworks and their respective guiding principles, serving as a basis for normative alignment.

AI systems must uphold transparency through explainability and traceability, fairness by mitigating bias, and privacy via secure data governance. Sustainability ensures long-term resilience without dependency, while inclusivity demands active engagement from affected communities to ensure cultural and contextual relevance.

1.2 From Logic to Responsibility: The Ethical Trajectory of AI

The formal emergence of artificial intelligence (AI) as a research field occurred in 1956 during the Dartmouth Summer Research Project on Artificial Intelligence [9]. Organized by McCarthy, Minsky, Shannon, and Rochester, this event marked the first time the term "artificial intelligence" was used and outlined the foundational assumptions of the field.

Artificial intelligence has increasingly permeated high-stakes domains of human life—such as judicial rulings, health diagnostics, and autonomous vehicles—raising urgent ethical

Table 1.1 Comparison of key ethical AI frameworks

Framework	Issuing organization	Core principles
USAID ethical AI	USAID [1]	Transparency, fairness, privacy, sustainability, inclusivity
OECD AI principles	OECD [2]	Inclusive growth, human-centered values, transparency, robustness, accountability
EU AI ethics guidelines	European commission AI HLEG [3]	Respect for autonomy, prevention of harm, fairness, explicability
UNESCO AI ethics recommendation	UNESCO [4]	Human rights, sustainability, cultural diversity, data governance, accountability
IEEE ethically aligned design	IEEE [5]	Well-being, accountability, transparency, human oversight
Singapore model AI framework	Singapore PDPC [6]	Explainability, fairness, robustness, human-centricity
UK CDEI AI framework	Centre for data ethics and innovation [7]	Transparency, fairness, accountability, contestability
Montréal declaration for responsible AI	Université de Montréal [8]	Well-being, autonomy, justice, privacy, democratic participation, equity, solidarity, sustainability, prudence, responsibility

challenges. In the justice system, AI tools like COMPAS have been shown to produce racially biased risk assessments, leading to concerns about due process, fairness, and explainability [10, 11]. The European Commission and the Council of Europe have emphasized the necessity of transparency and contestability in AI-assisted judicial decisions, warning that algorithmic opacity can undermine legal safeguards and human rights [12, 13]. In healthcare, AI is used for diagnostic support, treatment planning, and predictive analytics. However, studies have revealed that models trained on demographically imbalanced data can produce systematically inaccurate outcomes, especially for minority populations [14, 15]. The World Health Organization (WHO) and UNESCO have called for ethical principles that ensure non-discrimination, safety, and explainability in medical AI systems [3, 16]. In mobility, the deployment of autonomous vehicles raises moral and legal questions around accountability, accident liability, and decision-making in life-threatening scenarios. Ethical dilemmas such as those posed by "trolley problem" analogs have been widely discussed by ethicists and policy makers [17, 18]. The OECD and the UN have highlighted the need for robust frameworks to govern AI in transport, prioritizing human oversight and harm reduction. These examples illustrate that ethical concerns are not abstract but manifest concretely in systems that affect fundamental rights to liberty, health, and life. So, artificial intelligence has progressed from a speculative academic pursuit to a socio-technical force with profound implications across multiple domains of human such as judicial rulings, health diagnostics, and autonomous vehicles. However, in this new context, central concerns arise as autonomous decision-making, data privacy, algorithmic fairness, and systemic accountability [19, 20]. But, since early vision of AI, centered on symbolic reasoning and logic, was later expanded through works like Russell and Norvig's comprehensive textbook [21] and ethical frameworks such as AI4People [19], which address contemporary concerns about fairness, transparency, and safety in AI systems. Recent thinkers such as Hauser [22] continue to explore the implications of AI in human society, emphasizing both its potential and its risks. These issues are not merely technical challenges; they could reflect deeply rooted philosophical tensions concerning agency, justice, and responsibility in machine-mediated actions [23, 24]. Since then, the growing influence of AI in decision-making has catalyzed interdisciplinary efforts to embed ethical principles within technological systems and regulatory frameworks. Nevertheless, the discourse on AI ethics has evolved in parallel with historical technological milestones and global policy transformations [9, 25]:

The Early Years of AI (1950s–1970s)

Alan Turing, widely regarded as one of the founding figures of computer science, introduced in 1936 the concept of the "universal machine," later formalized as the Turing Machine [26]. This abstract model was capable of simulating the logic of any computer algorithm, laying the theoretical groundwork for modern digital computers.

In 1950, Turing extended his exploration of machine capabilities into the realm of cognition with the publication of his seminal paper *Computing Machinery and Intelligence* [27]. In this work, Turing posed the provocative question: "Can machines think?" and proposed the now-famous Turing Test to evaluate whether a machine can imitate human conversation convincingly.

In this test, a human interrogator interacts via text with both a human and a machine. If the interrogator cannot reliably distinguish the machine from the human, the machine is said to exhibit intelligent behavior. While this formulation was groundbreaking, it also introduced enduring ethical dilemmas. First, it frames intelligence as the capacity to imitate human behavior convincingly, potentially encouraging the development of deceptive systems whose outputs appear intelligent without genuine understanding [28]. Second, by focusing exclusively on external performance, the Turing Test sidesteps questions about consciousness, intentionality, or moral agency, reducing intelligence to surface-level simulation [29]. This reductionist view risks anthropomorphizing machines and undermines informed trust in human-AI interactions. As modern generative models increasingly pass variants of the Turing Test, these ethical concerns remain central: What does it mean to appear intelligent, and what obligations arise when machines convincingly simulate human-like cognition?

The AI Winter (1970s–1980s)

The first major AI winter, spanning the 1970s and 1980s, is often remembered as a time of technical stagnation and funding decline. However, this period also reveals important ethical concerns that continue to resonate today. Early AI researchers made ambitious promises about machines matching or surpassing human cognition [30], which shaped public policy and expectations. Yet, those promises often lacked epistemic humility and failed to disclose the limitations of symbolic systems and rule-based models [31]. This disconnect between technological optimism and actual capabilities led to misallocation of public funds, erosion of trust, and unrealistic societal expectations.

The ethical failure, then, lies not only in the inadequacy of algorithms or computing power, but in the lack of transparency and accountability in how AI progress was communicated to stakeholders—governments, funders, and the public [32]. Overpromising results in contexts where social outcomes are at stake—such as education, military applications, and governance—raises questions of responsibility and informed consent in technology development [23].

The Resurgence of AI: The 1980s and 1990s

The resurgence of AI during the 1980s and 1990s introduced not only technical innovations—such as expert systems and neural networks—but also the first signs of ethical tension in real-world deployment. The success of expert systems like XCON, which automated hardware configuration tasks at Digital Equipment Corporation, raised practical concerns about transparency, accountability, and professional trust [33]. These systems often failed to provide understandable justifications for their decisions, prompting early debates on explainability and responsibility in AI-assisted environments.

Simultaneously, philosophical critiques—such as John Searle's Chinese Room argument and Hubert Dreyfus' phenomenological stance—challenged the ethical assumption that syntactic manipulation of symbols could equate to genuine understanding [28, 29]. John Searle and Hubert Dreyfus introduced foundational ethical concerns about the nature of artificial intelligence. The "Chinese Room Argument," proposes a scenario in which a person who does not understand Chinese is locked in a room and follows a set of syntactic rules to respond to Chinese characters passed under the door. Although the outputs may appear meaningful to native speakers, the person inside has no understanding of the language—they are merely manipulating symbols. Searle argued that, likewise, computers executing formal algorithms do not "understand" in any meaningful sense—they simulate cognition without consciousness or intentionality [28]. Ethically, this calls into question the validity of attributing intelligence or moral agency to systems that lack genuine comprehension. In the same way, Hubert Dreyfus, influenced by Heidegger and Merleau-Ponty, argued that human intelligence is not reducible to rule-based logic but emerges from embodied experience and contextual engagement with the world. For Dreyfus, expertise involves intuition, familiarity, and physical interaction—dimensions that symbolic AI ignores [29]. The ethical implication is clear: over-relying on disembodied, rule-driven systems can result in misguided trust and poorly grounded decisions, especially in high-stakes domains like healthcare, law, or defense. These critiques warned against overestimating the capabilities of symbolic systems, emphasizing the need for ethical restraint in how AI is conceptualized and represented.

In the same decade, the rise of neural networks and backpropagation also introduced new ethical challenges. Unlike rule-based systems, connectionist models lacked interpretability, marking the beginning of a trade-off between performance and transparency that remains unresolved. The period also saw concerns about automation, labor displacement, and corporate control over AI technologies, raising early questions about the equitable distribution of AI's societal benefits [34].

The Modern AI Renaissance (2000-Present)

The modern resurgence of artificial intelligence has not only transformed technical capabilities but has also amplified ethical concerns regarding its design, deployment, and societal impact. As AI systems increasingly mediate access to services, influence decision-making, and automate critical processes, issues of fairness, accountability, transparency, and privacy have moved to the center of ethical discourse [5]. One of the most pressing challenges is the opacity of deep learning models, which function as "black boxes," making it difficult to explain or contest their outputs—especially in high-stakes fields such as healthcare, criminal justice, and finance [35]. This has led to a growing emphasis on Explainable AI (XAI), which seeks to render algorithmic decisions interpretable to human stakeholders [36].

Moreover, algorithmic bias—where historical inequalities embedded in data are replicated or amplified by AI systems—raises concerns about discrimination and structural injustice [37, 38]. Ethical frameworks have evolved to include not just individual rights but also collective and contextual harms, especially for marginalized communities [39]. In response, initiatives promoting fairness, accountability, and transparency (FAT) have emerged, calling for participatory, inclusive, and context-aware approaches to AI governance. These ethical concerns are now integral to global regulatory debates, such as the EU AI Act, which aims to establish binding requirements for trustworthy AI [13].

The discourse on AI ethics has evolved in parallel with historical technological milestones and global policy shifts. Since then, the growing influence of AI in public and private decision-making has prompted a convergence of philosophical reasoning, empirical research, and regulatory development, aiming to reconcile innovation with human values.

1.3 When AI Becomes a Decision-Maker

The increasing integration of artificial intelligence into decision-making processes marks a critical shift in the relationship between humans and machines. Traditionally, AI systems served as tools to support human judgment, offering recommendations or performing predefined tasks. However, modern AI systems—particularly those based on machine learning—are now entrusted with decisions that carry significant social, legal, and ethical implications [5, 40]. From determining creditworthiness and hiring outcomes to triaging patients or identifying criminal suspects, AI is no longer merely assisting humans, but in many cases, replacing or influencing human agency. This transition raises urgent ethical questions about accountability, transparency, and moral responsibility. When AI makes a harmful or discriminatory decision, who is to blame—the developer, the deployer, or the model itself? [41]. Scholars have warned that as algorithmic systems grow more complex and opaque, they can obscure the chain of responsibility, creating what has been called a "responsibility gap" [42]. Furthermore, delegating authority to machines may erode foundational legal and moral principles, such as due process, informed consent, and human dignity [19, 43].

Understanding AI as a decision-maker demands a reexamination of governance frameworks, not only to ensure fairness and accountability, but also to preserve the human values that underpin democratic and ethical institutions. This chapter explores the origins, implications, and challenges of this transition across multiple sectors, where AI's influence is no longer peripheral—but decisional.

1.3.1 AI for Social Good and Ethical Risks

The use of artificial intelligence (AI) for social good and sustainability has garnered strong support from influential scholars and practitioners who advocate for its transformative potential in addressing global challenges. Milind Tambe emphasizes the application of AI in public safety, wildlife conservation, and healthcare interventions, highlighting the effectiveness of predictive models in optimizing resource allocation in under-resourced communities [44]. Benedetta Brevini underscores the role of AI in mitigating climate change, enhancing energy efficiency, and promoting environmentally sustainable practices, while warning against unchecked techno-solutionism [45]. Amir Banifatemi promotes responsible innovation through global initiatives like the AI XPRIZE, positioning AI as a catalyst for economic inclusion and humanitarian progress [46]. Keolu Fox calls for ecologically sustainable AI development, advocating for the use of renewable energy and recycling practices to reduce the environmental footprint of large-scale computing infrastructures [47]. As a United Nations envoy, Amandeep Singh Gill emphasizes the importance of aligning AI development with international human rights frameworks and ethical governance [48].

Despite this optimism, numerous experts have raised concerns regarding the risks and unintended consequences of AI. Stephen Hawking famously warned that unregulated AI could surpass human intelligence and pose existential threats [49]. Yoshua Bengio has advocated for robust oversight mechanisms to prevent autonomous agents from acting beyond human control [50]. Sebastián Ríos has outlined risks including algorithmic manipulation, labor displacement, and systemic bias. Similarly, institutions such as the World Economic Forum [15] and the Inter-American Development Bank [51] have warned that, without appropriate safeguards, AI may exacerbate inequality and erode democratic accountability. Together, these perspectives converge on the need for strong governance frameworks, ethical oversight, and participatory approaches to ensure that AI technologies serve the public good without compromising human rights or societal cohesion.

1.3.2 Why High-Consequence AI Demands Rigorous Requirements

Classical software engineering is grounded in two foundational principles: *determinism*, the idea that software behaves predictably for a given input, and *code-level completeness*, the assumption that a system's behavior is fully defined by its source code and can be examined, tested, and verified [52]. This paradigm has enabled rigorous methods of specification, validation, and maintenance. However, contemporary AI systems—particularly those based on machine learning—undermine these foundations. Learning systems do not contain explicitly defined rules; instead, their decision-making capabilities emerge from statistical correlations in data, often via complex high-dimensional representations that defy intuitive understanding [53]. As a result, the same input may not always yield the same outcome due to stochastic training processes, and models may behave inconsistently across environments, especially when exposed to data distributions that differ from those seen during training.

The non-deterministic behavior of machine learning systems—stemming from stochastic training processes and data-dependent decision boundaries—amplifies the high-stakes risks summarized in Table 1.2. Because a model's outputs can shift when data distributions drift or when optimization landscapes converge to different local minima, neither designers nor auditors can guarantee identical results for identical inputs over time. This *epistemic opacity* [54] makes the ethical failures listed in the table—biased incarceration decisions in justice, misdiagnosis in health, and unintended civilian harm in defence—especially acute. Consequently, the *critical requirements* enumerated for each domain (fairness, robustness, oversight, etc.) must be treated as rigorous, lifecycle requirements, not after-the-fact desiderata.

This epistemological break introduces what Humphreys refers to as *epistemic opacity*—a condition in which it is not possible for human observers, even in principle, to fully reconstruct the internal reasoning of a computational system [54]. This poses significant ethical challenges: if designers cannot fully explain how a system arrives at a decision, how can we assign moral responsibility, establish accountability, or justify outcomes to

Table 1.2 Ethical risks and engineering challenges by domain

Domain	High-stakes risk	Critical requirements	Formal challenges
Justice	Biased incarceration decisions	Fairness, explainability, contestability	Specifying social fairness formally
Health	Misdiagnosis, treatment delays	Robustness, calibration, clinical traceability	Drift monitoring, runtime safety
Defence	Civilian casualties	Target discrimination, oversight, auditability	Norm formalization, causal traceability

affected stakeholders? [41]. The resulting "responsibility gap" [42] becomes especially problematic in high-stakes domains such as healthcare, finance, and criminal justice, where unjustified or biased decisions may have life-altering consequences. To mitigate these risks, researchers and institutions have proposed a shift from post hoc interpretability toward proactive engineering constraints that embed ethical safeguards into the AI lifecycle [19]. These include:

- (i) *formally specifiable requirements*, which involve defining machine behavior in mathematical terms, enabling verification techniques such as model checking or constraint propagation;
- (ii) *empirically monitorable requirements*, which require robust evaluation under real-world conditions, stress-testing models for performance across demographic groups or edge cases [56]; and
- (iii) *traceability*, which demands full documentation of datasets, training pipelines, model versions, and decision logs, making AI behavior auditable over time [57]. These properties are not merely technical features, but ethical imperatives in systems that increasingly govern human lives.

1.4 From Ethics to Engineering

AI systems increasingly mediate fundamental rights: to liberty, to health, to life. In these contexts, engineering becomes an instrument of justice. Hence, ethical principles such as fairness, safety, and transparency must be *encoded as verifiable requirements* and embedded within the IA development lifecycle.

In this way, Artificial intelligence systems are no longer merely technical tools: they operate in sensitive domains, demonstrating that AI does not simply process data; it intervenes in processes that shape civil liberties, access to essential services, and conditions of material existence. For instance, in the judicial system, certain algorithms are employed to assist in decisions related to parole and preventive detention. Likewise, in the healthcare sector, machine learning models play a role in aiding diagnoses, prioritizing treatments, and optimizing the distribution of hospital resources. Even in contexts like autonomous transportation or automated surveillance [58, 59], system decisions can affect physical integrity or human life.

On the other hand, while notions like fairness, safety, and transparency appear frequently in ethical guidelines for artificial intelligence, bringing these principles to life within real systems demands more than good intentions. It is not enough to name them—they must be woven into the very fabric of how systems are designed, built, and deployed. This means translating abstract ideals into concrete, testable requirements. Take fairness, for example, it is not simply a matter of proclaiming that a system should be fair. Developers must decide how to measure fairness in a given context—perhaps by comparing how the model behaves across different demographic groups, or by analyzing whether its errors fall disproportionately on specific populations. Similarly, the principle of safety goes beyond ensuring that a system works under ideal conditions; it calls for testing how the system holds up when things go wrong, when the data is noisy, incomplete, or unexpected. And with transparency, the demand is not just that the system be open to scrutiny, but that it be built in a way that allows others to trace how it works: through clear documentation, and through tools or methods that help users make sense of the system's decisions (Fig. 1.1).

1.5 Key Takeaways

1. **Ethics as a Technical Imperative**: AI systems are not ethically neutral; integrating ethics from design to deployment is vital for responsible innovation.
2. **From Logic to Responsibility**: The evolution from rule-based systems to machine learning introduces new moral challenges, requiring a shift from deterministic logic to context-sensitive accountability.
3. **High-Stakes Decision Making**: As AI systems increasingly influence socially impactful domains—such as healthcare, finance, and criminal justice—robust ethical frameworks must guide their development and use.
4. **AI for Social Good vs. Ethical Risks**: While AI holds transformative potential for public benefit, it simultaneously amplifies risks like bias, opacity, and harm at scale, demanding rigorous oversight.
5. **Engineering Ethics by Design**: Translating ethical principles into actionable engineering practices—such as fairness-aware algorithms, privacy-preserving learning, and transparency tools—is vital to operationalize trust.

Chapter 2 explores the historical and regulatory roots of ethical AI, from philosophical principles to the enforceable mandates of the European Union AI Act.

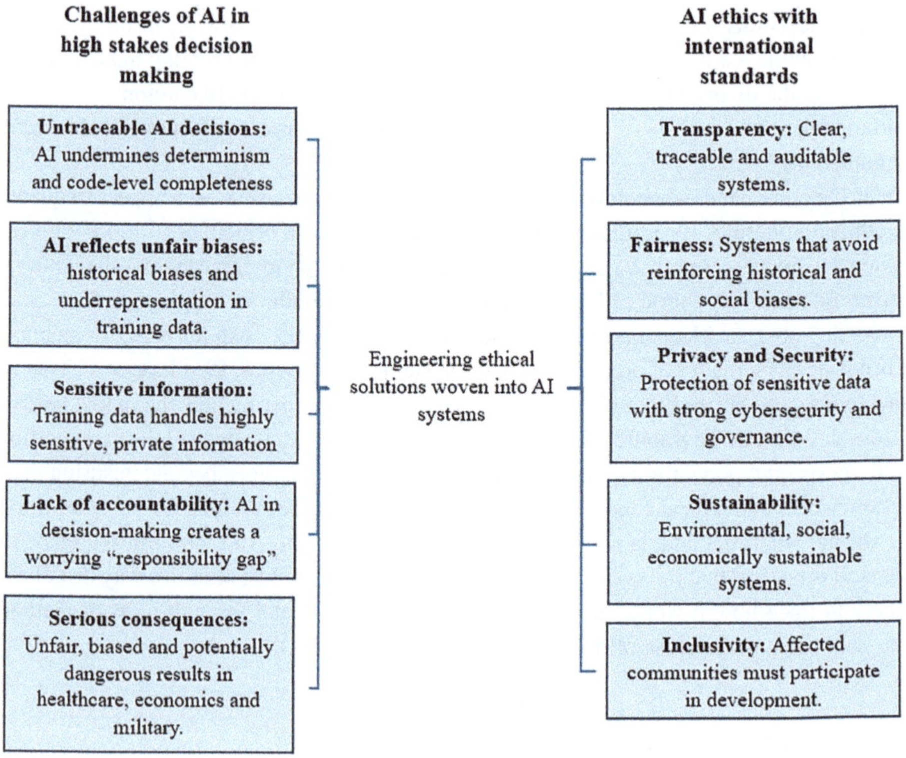

Fig. 1.1 Conceptual map of challenges of AI

References

1. USAID. (2023). *USAID AI Ethics Guide*. United States Agency for International Development. Retrieved from https://cdn.prod.website-files.com/63b7f45933958e6d310604b1/657aa4c38a08d605d1f2daba__USAID
2. OECD. (2019). *OECD Principles on Artificial Intelligence*. Organisation for Economic Co-operation and Development. Retrieved from https://www.oecd.org/going-digital/ai/principles/
3. European Commission AI HLEG. (2019). *Ethics Guidelines for Trustworthy AI*. High-Level Expert Group on AI, European Commission. Retrieved from https://ec.europa.eu/newsroom/dae/document.cfm?doc_id=60419
4. UNESCO. (2021). *Recommendation on the Ethics of Artificial Intelligence*. United Nations Educational, Scientific and Cultural Organization. Retrieved from https://unesdoc.unesco.org/ark:/48223/pf0000381137
5. IEEE. (2019). *Ethically Aligned Design: A Vision for Prioritizing Human Well-being with Autonomous and Intelligent Systems*. IEEE Standards Association. Retrieved from https://ethicsinaction.ieee.org/

6. Singapore PDPC. (2020). *Model AI Governance Framework*. Personal Data Protection Commission Singapore. Retrieved from https://www.pdpc.gov.sg/policies-and-guidelines/model-ai-governance-framework
7. Centre for Data Ethics and Innovation. (2020). *The CDEI AI Barometer*. UK Government. Retrieved from https://www.gov.uk/government/collections/cdei-ai-barometer
8. Université de Montréal. (2018). *Montréal Declaration for a Responsible Development of Artificial Intelligence*. Retrieved from https://www.montrealdeclaration-responsibleai.com/
9. McCarthy, J., Minsky, M. L., Rochester, N., Shannon, C. E.: A Proposal for the Dartmouth Summer Research Project on Artificial Intelligence. Dartmouth College, Hanover, NH (2006)
10. Angwin, J., Larson, J., Mattu, S., & Kirchner, L. (2016, mayo 23). Machine Bias: There's software used across the country to predict future criminals. And it's biased against blacks. ProPublica. https://www.propublica.org/article/machine-bias-risk-assessments-in-criminal-sentencing
11. O'Neil, C.: Weapons of Math Destruction: How Big Data Increases Inequality and Threatens Democracy. Crown Publishing Group, New York (2016)
12. Council of Europe, European Commission for the Efficiency of Justice (CEPEJ). (2019). European ethical charter on the use of artificial intelligence in judicial systems and their environment (adoptado en Strasbourg, 3–4 diciembre 2018). https://www.europarl.europa.eu/cmsdata/196205/COUNCIL
13. European Commission: Proposal for a Regulation Laying Down Harmonised Rules on Artificial Intelligence (Artificial Intelligence Act), COM(2021) 206 final (2021)
14. Obermeyer, Z., Powers, B., Vogeli, C., Mullainathan, S.: Dissecting Racial Bias in an Algorithm Used to Manage the Health of Populations. Science **366**(6464), 447–453 (2019)
15. Rajkomar, A., Hardt, M., Howell, M.D., Corrado, G., Chin, M.H.: Ensuring Fairness in Machine Learning to Advance Health Equity. Annals of Internal Medicine **169**(12), 866–872 (2018)
16. World Health Organization: Ethics and Governance of Artificial Intelligence for Health: WHO Guidance. Geneva (2021)
17. Bonnefon, J.F., Shariff, A., Rahwan, I.: The Social Dilemma of Autonomous Vehicles. Science **352**(6293), 1573–1576 (2016)
18. High-Level Expert Group on AI: Ethics Guidelines for Trustworthy AI. European Commission (2019)
19. Floridi, L., Cowls, J., Beltrametti, M., Chatila, R., Chazerand, P., Dignum, V., et al.: AI4People—An Ethical Framework for a Good AI Society: Opportunities, Risks, Principles, and Recommendations. *Minds and Machines* **28**(4), 689–707 (2018)
20. Binns, R.: Fairness in Machine Learning: Lessons from Political Philosophy. Proceedings of the 2018 Conference on Fairness, Accountability, and Transparency, 149–159 (2018)
21. Russell, S. J., Norvig, P.: Artificial Intelligence: A Modern Approach (4th ed.). *Pearson* (2020)
22. Mitchell, M. (s. f.). Artificial Intelligence: A Guide for Thinking Humans (página del autor). Recuperado de https://melaniemitchell.me/aibook/
23. Moor, J.H.: The Nature, Importance, and Difficulty of Machine Ethics. IEEE Intelligent Systems **21**(4), 18–21 (2006)
24. Cath, C.: Governing Artificial Intelligence: Ethical, Legal and Technical Opportunities and Challenges. Philosophical Transactions of the Royal Society A **376**(2133), 20180080 (2018)
25. Crevier, D. (1993). AI: The tumultuous history of the search for artificial intelligence. Basic Books. https://www.amazon.com/Ai-Tumultuous-History-Artificial-Intelligence/dp/0465029973
26. Turing, A. M.: On Computable Numbers, with an Application to the Entscheidungsproblem. *Proceedings of the London Mathematical Society* **2**(42), 230–265 (1936)
27. Turing, A.M.: Computing Machinery and Intelligence. Mind **59**(236), 433–460 (1950)
28. Searle, J. R. (1980). Minds, brains, and programs. Behavioral and Brain Sciences, 3(3), 417–424. https://doi.org/10.1017/S0140525X00005756

29. Dreyfus, H.L.: What Computers Still Can't Do: A Critique of Artificial Reason. MIT Press, Cambridge (1992)
30. Simon, H.A.: The Shape of Automation for Men and Management. Harper and Row, New York (1965)
31. Dreyfus, H.L.: What Computers Can't Do: A Critique of Artificial Reason. Harper and Row, New York (1972)
32. Lighthill, J.: Artificial Intelligence: A General Survey. In: Artificial Intelligence: A Paper Symposium, Science Research Council (UK), London (1973)
33. Shortliffe, E. H. (1976). Computer-based medical consultations: MYCIN. Elsevier. https://doi.org/10.1016/B978-0-444-00179-5.X5001-X
34. Weizenbaum, J. (1976). Computer power and human reason: From judgment to calculation. W. H. Freeman and Company.
35. Arrieta, A.B., et al.: Explainable Artificial Intelligence (XAI): Concepts, Taxonomies, Opportunities and Challenges toward Responsible AI. Information Fusion **58**, 82–115 (2020)
36. Doshi-Velez, F., Kim, B.: Towards A Rigorous Science of Interpretable Machine Learning. arXiv preprint arXiv:1702.08608 (2017)
37. Eubanks, V.: Automating Inequality: How High-Tech Tools Profile, Police, and Punish the Poor. St. Martin's Press, New York (2018)
38. O'Neil, C.: Weapons of Math Destruction: How Big Data Increases Inequality and Threatens Democracy. Crown Publishing Group, New York (2016)
39. Birhane, A.: Algorithmic Injustices: Towards a Relational Ethics. In: Proceedings of the 2021 ACM Conference on Fairness, Accountability, and Transparency, pp. 389–400 (2021)
40. Jobin, A., Ienca, M., Vayena, E.: The Global Landscape of AI Ethics Guidelines. Nature Machine Intelligence **1**(9), 389–399 (2019)
41. Burrell, J.: How the Machine 'Thinks': Understanding Opacity in Machine Learning Algorithms. Big Data & Society **3**(1), 1–12
42. Matthias, A.: The Responsibility Gap: Ascribing Responsibility for the Actions of Learning Automata. Ethics and Information Technology **6**(3), 175–183 (2004)
43. Binns, R.: Fairness in Machine Learning: Lessons from Political Philosophy. Proceedings of the 2018 Conference on Fairness, Accountability and Transparency (FAT*), 149–159 (2018)
44. Association of Pacific Rim Universities. (2020). Artificial intelligence for social good (Informe). https://www.apru.org/wp-content/uploads/2020/09/layout_v3_web_page.pdf
45. Petersen, E. (2022). [Review of Is AI Good for the Planet?, by B. Brevini]. Prometheus, 38(2), 246–250. https://www.jstor.org/stable/48682293
46. McGregor, S. (2023). A scaled multiyear responsible artificial intelligence impact assessment. Computer, 56(8), 20–27. https://doi.org/10.1109/MC.2022.3231551
47. Khurana, S. (2025). Decolonizing artificial intelligence: Indigenous knowledge systems, epistemic pluralism, and the ethics of technology. Journal of Computer Allied Intelligence, 3(3), 1–10. https://doi.org/10.69996/jcai.2025013
48. Gill, A.S., Germann, S. Conceptual and normative approaches to AI governance for a global digital ecosystem supportive of the UN Sustainable Development Goals (SDGs). AI Ethics 2, 293–301 (2022). https://doi.org/10.1007/s43681-021-00058-z
49. Cambridge University. (2016, 19 de octubre). "The best or worst thing to happen to humanity" – Stephen Hawking launches Centre for the Future of Intelligence. University of Cambridge. https://www.cam.ac.uk/research/news/the-best-or-worst-thing-to-happen-to-humanity-stephen-hawking-launches-centre-for-the-future-of
50. Sayles, J. (2024). Human Oversight of AI Systems. In: Principles of AI Governance and Model Risk Management. Apress, Berkeley, CA. https://doi.org/10.1007/979-8-8688-0983-5_12
51. Inter-American Development Bank: Artificial Intelligence and Ethics in Latin America. Washington, D.C. (2020)

52. D. L. Parnas. 1972. On the criteria to be used in decomposing systems into modules. Commun. ACM 15, 12 (Dec. 1972), 1053–1058. https://doi.org/10.1145/361598.361623
53. Lipton, Z.C.: The Mythos of Model Interpretability. Communications of the ACM **61**(10), 36–43 (2018)
54. Humphreys, P.: The Philosophical Novelty of Computer Simulation Methods. Synthese **169**(3), 615–626 (2009)
55. Chihani, Z. (2021). Formal methods for AI: Lessons from the past, promises of the future (CAID 2021). HAL Open Archive. https://hal.science/hal-04479570v1
56. Raji, I. D., Smart, A., White, R. N., Mitchell, M., Gebru, T., Hutchinson, B., Smith-Loud, J., Theron, D., & Barnes, P. (2020). Closing the AI accountability gap: Defining an end-to-end framework for internal algorithmic auditing. En Proceedings of the 2020 Conference on Fairness, Accountability, and Transparency (FAT '20)* (pp. 33–44). Association for Computing Machinery. https://doi.org/10.1145/3351095.3372873
57. Mitchell, M., Wu, S., Zaldivar, A., Barnes, P., Vasserman, L., Hutchinson, B., et al.: Model Cards for Model Reporting. In: Proceedings of the Conference on Fairness, Accountability, and Transparency (FAT*), pp. 220–229 (2019)
58. Carbonell, M., Sallari Rivera, J., & Santivañez Muñoz, J. (2025). Artificial intelligence in video surveillance systems for suspicious activity detection and incident response: A systematic review. Advances in Science and Technology Research Journal, 19(3), 389–405. https://doi.org/10.12913/22998624/196795
59. Lin, J., Zou, C., Lan, L., Luo, Y., Yu, Y., Wang, Y., ... and Tian, Y. (2025). Towards to real world vehicle privacy protection: A new dataset and benchmark. Pattern Recognition, 111918.

2 From Philosophy to Regulation: The Global Evolution of AI Ethics

2.1 From Aspirations to Obligations

The ethical regulation of technology has historically been rooted in normative frameworks designed to constrain the misuse of power and preserve human dignity—whether through the Hippocratic Oath in medicine, the Geneva Conventions in warfare, or professional codes in engineering. These traditions assume that moral responsibility lies with human agents capable of judgment and accountability. However, the contemporary rise of artificial intelligence (AI)—particularly systems that are autonomous, data-driven, and opaque—challenges this assumption at its core. AI systems increasingly make decisions that affect legal outcomes, access to healthcare, employment, and physical safety. As a result, ethical considerations can no longer remain aspirational or advisory; they must evolve into formal, enforceable obligations encoded into the design, development, and deployment of AI systems [1, 2]. This transition from ethical *intentions* to technical *obligations* is driven by what philosophers and ethicists have described as the problem of *epistemic opacity* [3]: the idea that many machine learning systems are so complex, dynamic, and non-deterministic that even their creators cannot fully explain how decisions are made [4].

Epistemic opacity refers to the inability to understand all the relevant elements of a computational process. For instance, consider a highly advanced calculator that produces a correct result, but follows a sequence of steps so intricate or concealed that the user cannot reconstruct how it reached the answer. In this case, the process is epistemically opaque—even if the output is technically correct, there is no clear way to fully explain or verify how it was generated. This concept is central to evaluating the transparency and reliability of complex systems.

The challenge becomes even more pronounced in the case of large language models (LLMs) deployed in high-stakes domains such as medical diagnosis or legal decision-making. In these contexts, the system's outputs—clinical suggestions, legal arguments,

R. Andrade et al., *Building Ethical and Secure AI*, Synthesis Lectures on Computer Science,
https://doi.org/10.1007/978-3-032-25789-5_2

or verdict recommendations—may appear accurate or useful, yet the underlying reasoning remains largely inaccessible to users. Because of their vast complexity and non-deterministic behavior, even the developers of LLMs are often unable to precisely explain how specific responses are formed. This lack of interpretability raises serious concerns about accountability, reliability, and trust—especially when such systems influence decisions that directly affect human well-being and legal rights. To address this, ethics must be embedded throughout the AI lifecycle as a set of verifiable and auditable requirements—such as explainability, fairness, robustness, and traceability [5, 6]. This approach marks a paradigmatic shift: from viewing ethics as external to computation, to treating it as an intrinsic component of socio-technical system design.

2.1.1 Early Ethical Foundations and Fictional Precedents

The ethical regulation of intelligent machines has precursors not only in applied philosophy and engineering codes, but also in cultural imagination and anticipatory discourse. This section explores how early conceptualizations—both fictional and institutional—provided initial frameworks to address the moral responsibilities associated with artificial agents, even before the existence of general-purpose AI.

Science Fiction and Theoretical Precedents

A landmark example of anticipatory ethical reasoning is found in Isaac Asimov's "Three Laws of Robotics," which attempted to encode normative constraints into robotic behavior:

1. not harming humans,
2. obeying orders unless it conflicts with the first law, and
3. protecting one's own existence unless it conflicts with the first two [7].

Although these laws were purely fictional, they highlight enduring challenges in formalizing ethical imperatives in computational systems: ambiguity in natural language formulations, conflicting priorities, and a lack of contextual adaptability. Scholars have since shown that even simple ethical rules can lead to unintended consequences in multi-agent environments, especially where trade-offs between fairness, safety, and autonomy arise [8]. In the paper *"The Nature, Importance, and Difficulty of Machine Ethics"* [9], James Moor proposed a foundational classification of machine ethics by articulating four categories of ethical agency based on a machine's capacity to engage with moral reasoning. These are:

1. ***Ethical Impact Agents***: Any machine whose actions can be evaluated for their ethical consequences, even if it was not designed with ethical reasoning capabilities. For exam-

ple, a self-driving car that causes harm can be assessed ethically regardless of its internal architecture.

2. ***Implicit Ethical Agents***: Machines that are explicitly designed to avoid unethical outcomes. These agents incorporate safeguards and constraints to prevent harm or bias, such as medical devices programmed with strict safety protocols.
3. ***Explicit Ethical Agents***: Machines that can reason about ethical situations. They are capable of analyzing moral dilemmas, applying ethical principles, and selecting justified actions based on such reasoning.
4. ***Full Ethical Agents***: Machines with advanced or hypothetical autonomy that can make explicit moral judgments and justify them, potentially comparable to human-level ethical reasoning and responsibility.

Despite these limitations, Asimov's framework introduced a valuable lens for considering machine agency and responsibility—topics now central to AI ethics. Ethical risk assessment is widely regarded as a cornerstone of ethical governance. However, on its own, it is not sufficient—particularly in the case of *implicit ethical agents*. One of the core ethical principles outlined in *Ethically Aligned Design* [10] emphasizes the importance of transparency: it should always be possible to understand how and why an autonomous system arrived at a particular decision. However, Transparency is not an inherent property of autonomous systems. Instead, it must be deliberately engineered, through the integration of subsystems capable of securely logging inputs, outputs, and decision-making processes—functionally equivalent to an aircraft's flight data recorder [8]. Without such mechanisms, uncovering the causes of failures becomes nearly impossible. For example, in the aftermath of a driverless car accident or a medical misdiagnosis by an AI system, the absence of transparency hampers any effort to determine what went wrong. This traceability is essential for addressing faults, ensuring safety, and establishing accountability [11].

Machine Morality

- Can an AI system be considered a moral agent?
- Should we ascribe any kind of "moral responsibility" to algorithms?

2.1.2 Professional Codes and the Rise of Ethical Frameworks

Beginning in the late twentieth century, professional bodies such as the Association for Computing Machinery (ACM) and the Institute of Electrical and Electronics Engineers (IEEE) published ethical guidelines emphasizing core values such as accountability, privacy, non-discrimination, and transparency [10, 12]. These documents function as aspirational norms that reflect the ethical commitments of the engineering community. However, they suffer from two critical limitations:

1. They lack normative enforceability. Compliance is typically voluntary, and there are limited mechanisms for sanctioning unethical design or deployment practices.
2. They lack semantic operationalization: the principles stated are not directly translatable into technical requirements, system specifications, or testable properties [5].

This semantic gap weakens the ability of these codes to guide real-world development or to be integrated into automated verification pipelines. In response to these shortcomings, recent organizations advocate for a shift from abstract values to implementable ethical frameworks, involving regulatory oversight, algorithmic impact assessments, and the integration of normative constraints directly into the system lifecycle [2, 11]. This movement acknowledges that without formal integration, ethics remains peripheral—symbolically important but functionally inert.

The consolidation of AI ethics as a formal domain has been marked by the emergence of influential frameworks that reflect diverse priorities across technical, social, and policy dimensions. As illustrated in Table 2.1, the 2016 IEEE Global Initiative was among the first engineering-driven efforts to embed ethical values—such as well-being, accountability, and transparency—into the system design lifecycle [10]. This was soon followed by the 2017 Asilomar Principles, which provided philosophical and technical guidelines emphasizing safety, alignment, and human oversight in advanced AI research [13]. In 2018, the Montréal Declaration expanded the ethical discourse by explicitly integrating principles of social justice, inclusivity, and democratic participation [8]. Finally, the 2019 OECD AI Principles marked a milestone in international governance by securing intergovernmental consensus on values such as robustness, fairness, and human-centeredness in AI systems [14]. Together, these initiatives represent a progressive shift from voluntary professional codes to globally coordinated ethical norms, and underscore the necessity of translating abstract principles into actionable governance and design practices.

Table 2.1 Selected milestones in AI ethics frameworks

Year	Initiative	Contribution
2016	IEEE global initiative	Engineering-centric ethical design principles
2017	Asilomar principles	Research guidelines for alignment, human control
2018	Montréal declaration	Emphasis on social justice, inclusivity
2019	OECD AI principles	Intergovernmental policy convergence on ethical AI

2.1.3 International Guidelines: From IEEE to UNESCO

As artificial intelligence systems become increasingly integrated into critical societal functions, a range of international initiatives have emerged to establish ethical principles and governance frameworks. These initiatives differ in scope, enforceability, and origin, but collectively form the foundation for responsible AI development. This subsection surveys key milestones and guidelines that have shaped global discourse.

IEEE Global Initiative on Ethically Aligned Design (2016) The IEEE's 2016 initiative was a pioneering effort to infuse ethics directly into the engineering of autonomous and intelligent systems. It introduced the notion of "Ethically Aligned Design," focusing on human well-being, accountability, transparency, and value-sensitive design as core principles. It marked a shift toward normative requirements embedded in technical development.

Asilomar AI Principles (2017) Developed by leading AI researchers under the Future of Life Institute, the Asilomar Principles comprise 23 high-level recommendations related to research transparency, long-term safety, value alignment, and human control. Though voluntary, these principles gained broad support and catalyzed discussions about existential risks and governance of advanced AI systems.

Montréal Declaration for a Responsible Development of AI (2018) The Montréal Declaration, a Canadian-led initiative, articulated ethical commitments grounded in social justice, equity, and democratic participation. It emphasized inclusivity, protection of vulnerable groups, and the importance of public engagement in shaping AI's trajectory.

OECD AI Principles (2019) Adopted by over 40 countries, the OECD AI Principles represent a rare intergovernmental consensus on AI governance. They advocate for human-centered values, transparency, robustness, and accountability. These principles influenced other frameworks such as the EU AI Act and national strategies around the world.

EU AI Ethics Guidelines (HLEG) (2019) Preceding the binding EU AI Act, the High-Level Expert Group's 2019 guidelines laid out seven requirements for trustworthy AI: human agency, technical robustness, privacy and data governance, transparency, diversity and non-discrimination, societal well-being, and accountability. These guidelines served as a soft-law precursor to regulatory developments.

UNESCO AI Ethics Recommendation (2021) UNESCO's recommendation is the first global normative instrument on AI ethics, adopted unanimously by 193 member states. It highlights gender equality, environmental sustainability, data protection, and cultural diversity, with a strong emphasis on bridging digital divides and enhancing capacity-building in the Global South.

G7 Hiroshima AI Principles (2023) The G7 Hiroshima Process responded to the rapid advancement of generative AI and foundation models. It emphasized guiding principles such as transparency, security, fairness, and international cooperation. Although non-binding, these principles influence national regulations and industry standards.

2.2 Risk-Based Governance and Global Regulatory Models

In recent years, there has been a marked transition in global AI governance from aspirational ethical declarations to pragmatic risk-management frameworks. This shift reflects a growing consensus that while ethical values such as fairness, transparency, and accountability remain crucial, their enforcement must be grounded in engineering principles and institutional mechanisms that manage concrete risks. As argued by Mittelstadt [6], ethical AI must move beyond value articulation toward procedural implementation, particularly in high-stakes domains where failures can lead to tangible harm.

World Economic Forum: Model Governance Framework (2023) The WEF's framework addresses AI risk through a multi-stakeholder approach, promoting collaborative risk mitigation involving governments, industry, and civil society [15]. It identifies key risk vectors—algorithmic bias, system malfunction, lack of explainability—and proposes practical mitigation strategies like ethics impact assessments and dynamic monitoring systems. It complements legal instruments by offering agile governance tools that can be rapidly adapted to emerging technologies.

OECD Framework for Risk-Based Classification of AI Systems (2021) The OECD proposed a taxonomy that classifies AI systems based on impact, autonomy, and context of deployment [14]. It encourages member states to adopt proportionate regulatory responses, providing a basis for intergovernmental harmonization. The framework incorporates concepts like human-centricity and accountability and supports the development of audit mechanisms, especially for high-risk applications in finance, mobility, and labor markets.

United States: NIST AI Risk Management Framework (2023) The United States' 2023 NIST AI Risk Management Framework exemplifies the operationalization of trustworthiness through a lifecycle-based approach. This framework articulates core functions—Map, Measure, Manage, and Govern—that support organizations in proactively addressing risks posed by AI systems [16]. It emphasizes socio-technical dimensions, including privacy, robustness, and resilience, and provides practical guidelines and an accompanying Playbook to contextualize implementation across sectors. Notably, it treats AI risk as a function of both technical and organizational factors, recognizing the opacity and emergent behavior of modern AI systems.

China: Risk Management through State-Centric Governance China's approach to AI risk is grounded in regulatory control over generative content, platform accountability, and the strategic alignment of AI with national interests [17]. The 2022 regulations on recommendation algorithms and generative AI mandate pre-registration, explainability, and conformity with "socialist core values." While this model lacks transparency in enforcement, it prioritizes risk dimensions associated with misinformation, social stability, and ideological coherence. Scholars such as Creemers [18] highlight how China's risk-based governance is embedded in a broader framework of cyber-sovereignty and centralized oversight.

European Union: The AI Act (2024/1689) The European Union's AI Act represents the most comprehensive regulatory effort to date, categorizing AI systems into four tiers of risk:

unacceptable, high, limited, and minimal. High-risk systems—such as those in healthcare, law enforcement, and education—must comply with strict engineering obligations, including data governance, human oversight, and robustness guarantees [19]. These requirements are designed to mitigate epistemic opacity and ensure traceability. The Act embodies a shift from voluntary codes to enforceable legal duties, underscoring the EU's commitment to human rights and safety.

ISO/IEC 23894:2023—AI Risk Management The ISO/IEC 23894:2023 standard offers an international guideline for managing AI-specific risks across the lifecycle of a system [20]. Aligned with ISO 31000, it addresses both technical (model failure, data drift) and social (bias, exclusion) hazards. The framework supports the identification, assessment, and control of uncertain outcomes associated with AI operations, especially in critical infrastructures. Its emphasis on documentation, accountability, and interoperability makes it suitable for multinational environments.

Singapore: Model AI Governance Framework (2020/2022) Singapore's Model AI Governance Framework, issued by the PDPC, focuses on managing risks through corporate governance mechanisms and sectoral guidance. It integrates principles of transparency, fairness, and accountability into organizational processes, offering a risk-based Assessment Toolkit that helps companies evaluate the proportionality of risk and mitigation strategies [21]. While voluntary, its widespread adoption in the Asia-Pacific region signals a trend toward standardizing risk-sensitive AI practices in the private sector.

Taken together, these frameworks reflect a growing sophistication in how the international community addresses AI risks. They share an emphasis on context-sensitive classification, ongoing oversight, and enforceable standards, marking a decisive shift from ethical intent to risk-based regulation. To contextualize the diversity of global approaches to AI risk governance, Table 2.2 presents a comparative overview of major international frameworks. These include regulatory instruments such as the European Union's AI Act, technical standards like ISO/IEC 23894:2023, and policy-driven initiatives from organizations such as the NIST, OECD, and the World Economic Forum. The table highlights key dimensions including their reliance on risk-based classification, level of enforceability, and degree of technical integration. This comparative lens underscores the evolving landscape of AI regulation and the varying degrees to which ethical principles are operationalized across jurisdictions.

The ethical implementation of AI systems often requires balancing competing priorities. A common tension arises between **accuracy**—the model's ability to make correct predictions—and **fairness**, which ensures that outcomes do not disadvantage specific social groups.

Table 2.2 Comparative table of risk-based AI governance frameworks

Framework/ Organization	Risk-based approach	Enforceability	Technical integration
NIST AI RMF (USA)	Yes—Emphasizes contextual risk assessment and mitigation	Voluntary/ Informative	High—Lifecycle-based tools and mappings
EU AI act	Yes—Tiered classification (Unacceptable, High, Limited, Minimal)	Legally binding (in EU)	High—Requires traceability, data governance, risk mgmt
China's AI framework	Partially—Focused on state security, social harmony, limited transparency	State-Enforced (Top-down)	Medium—Focus on implementation via state platforms
ISO/IEC 23894:2023	Yes—Technical guidance for AI risk-management lifecycle	Voluntary standard (ISO)	High—Lifecycle focus, metrics, and validation
Singapore model AI Governance	Yes—Encourages risk and impact assessments	Advisory	Medium—Encourages best practices
OECD classification	Yes—Taxonomy to assess impact and autonomy	Advisory	Low—Conceptual classification
WEF AI governance	Yes—Holistic view integrating risk, ethics, and operations	Advisory	Medium—Operationalization tools suggested

2.3 From Principles to Formal Verification

2.3.1 Mapping Ethics to Technical Properties

One of the central challenges in aligning artificial intelligence (AI) systems with ethical imperatives is translating high-level values into concrete, verifiable properties. Table 2.3 presents a structured mapping between widely recognized ethical principles and their corresponding formal representations and verification techniques. This operationalization is critical to ensure that ethical claims about AI systems can be substantiated with computational rigor and engineering discipline.

Fairness is commonly represented through statistical and group-based metrics such as Equalized Odds, Individual Fairness, and Group Parity. These abstractions allow system behaviors to be audited and evaluated using SMT solvers, formal audits, or statistical validation methods. This ensures that machine learning models do not reinforce or amplify social biases, especially in domains like hiring or criminal justice.

Safety, a cornerstone in critical systems, is encoded via invariants, fail-safe mechanisms, and hazard logs. Verification tools such as model checking and runtime verification are

Table 2.3 Mapping principles to formal properties

Ethical principle	Formal representation	Verification techniques
Fairness	Equalized odds, Individual fairness, Group parity	SMT solvers, formal audits, statistical analysis
Safety	Invariants, fail-safe guards, hazard logs	Model checking, runtime verification
Privacy	Differential privacy, role-based access control	Formal type systems, policy logics
Explainability	Argument graphs, justification rules	Logical traceability, explainable-by-design models
Human oversight	Temporal constraints on autonomy	TLA^{+} contracts, hybrid symbolic models

employed to assess whether a system operates within acceptable risk boundaries, particularly under unforeseen circumstances.

Privacy is approached through technical frameworks like differential privacy and role-based access control (RBAC). These mechanisms are validated using formal type systems and policy logics, ensuring that personal data is accessed and processed in compliance with both legal standards and user expectations.

Explainability addresses the societal need for transparency in algorithmic decisions. By formalizing justification structures through argument graphs and rule-based explanations, designers can implement traceability pipelines and design-for-explanation mechanisms that allow for post hoc and ex ante assessments.

Human Oversight, finally, is ensured by embedding temporal constraints on autonomy. Tools such as TLA^{+} contracts and hybrid symbolic models guarantee that human operators retain meaningful control and accountability pathways over autonomous decision-making systems.

Together, these formal frameworks constitute a methodological bridge from intentions to obligations, reinforcing that ethical AI must not only be aspirational but also computationally enforceable and verifiable.

The Autonomous Car Dilemma

- Who should be responsible for an accident: the manufacturer, the programmer, or the algorithm?
- Does the answer change if the system decides to sacrifice one life to save many?

2.3.2 Theoretical Foundations: Formal Methods

Ethical Foundations

Norbert Wiener, often regarded as the father of cybernetics, was among the first to warn about the moral obligations tied to autonomous systems capable of adaptation and feedback. His vision laid the groundwork for embedding safety, human oversight, and social responsibility into the design of intelligent machines [22]. Decades later, Floridi and Cowls expanded this foundation by formulating a normative framework for AI ethics centered on five principles: beneficence, non-maleficence, autonomy, justice, and explicability [11]. These principles function not merely as aspirational goals but as actionable guidelines to align technical development with human values across the AI lifecycle.

Legal Accountability and Transparency

Lehr and Ohm argued that opaque algorithmic systems threaten democratic principles such as transparency and due process. They advocate for auditability and retrospective traceability mechanisms to ensure algorithmic accountability [23]. In parallel, Binns emphasized the need to operationalize the legal "right to an explanation"—enshrined in data protection laws like the GDPR—through practical tools such as logical transparency artefacts, argumentation graphs, and interpretable workflows [11]. These views converge on the necessity of embedding institutional safeguards within AI development to ensure fairness and recourse for affected individuals.

Verification Techniques and Technical

Bridging the ethical with the technical, Floridi's contributions promote the integration of ethical reasoning into system design using formal methods [11]. Temporal logic systems, such as TLA+, are used to specify and verify human oversight and safety properties in AI pipelines. Additionally, satisfiability modulo theories (SMT) solvers support legal and fairness verification in automated decision-making [23]. Complementing these, Explainable AI (XAI) techniques—like SHAP, LIME, and logical explanation graphs—enhance interpretability and allow external audits, thereby reinforcing transparency and trustworthiness [11].

These theoretical contributions collectively support the shift from abstract ethical intentions to the design of formal engineering artefacts that encode those norms. They also form the philosophical and methodological basis for regulatory frameworks such as ISO/IEC 23894 (AI Risk Management) and the European Union's AI Act (2024/1689), both of which mandate traceable, verifiable, and explainable system properties in high-risk AI applications. As such, formalization enables not only rigorous internal design standards but also compliance with emerging international norms for trustworthy and accountable AI systems (Fig. 2.1).

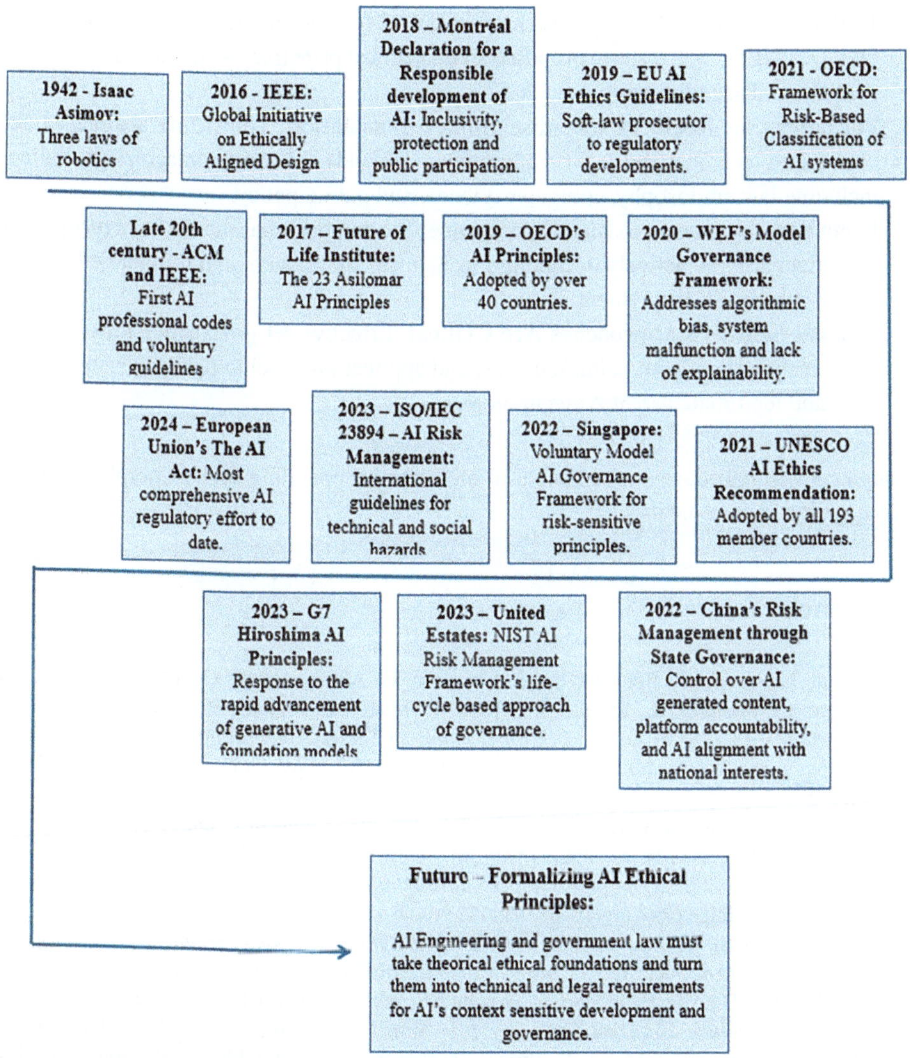

Fig. 2.1 Conceptual map ethical AI guidelines

2.4 Key Takeaways

1. **Ethical Principles Have Evolved Toward Obligations**. The development of AI ethics has shifted from aspirational and voluntary frameworks to enforceable norms and legal standards, reflecting the urgency of mitigating AI's societal risks.

2. **Global Guidelines Attempt Harmonization**. Multiple international initiatives (e.g., OECD, UNESCO, EU) have proposed shared ethical principles—such as fairness, transparency, and accountability.
3. **Formalization Requires Interdisciplinary Translation**. Translating abstract ethical values into technical and legal requirements demands collaboration across disciplines, including law, philosophy, computer science, and public policy.
4. **From Risk Awareness to Risk Governance**. The emphasis has moved from recognizing potential harms to actively designing mechanisms that govern and mitigate ethical and safety risks in AI deployment.
5. **Context-Sensitive Approaches Are Critical**. Effective AI governance must consider socio-technical context, cultural norms, and application-specific risks to ensure responsible and legitimate use of AI technologies.

Chapter 3 will introduce mathematical frameworks for encoding such principles into verifiable system requirements.

References

1. Floridi, L., Cowls, J., Beltrametti, M., Chiarello, F., Alemanno, A., Chatila, R., Dignum, V., Luetge, C., Madelin, R., Pagallo, U., Rossi, F., Shafer, B., Valcke, P., & Vayena, E. (2018). *AI4People—An Ethical Framework for a Good AI Society: Opportunities, Risks, Principles, and Recommendations*. Minds and Machines, 28, 689–707. https://doi.org/10.1007/s11023-018-9482-5
2. Jobin, A., Ienca, M., & Vayena, E. (2019). *The global landscape of AI ethics guidelines*. Nature Machine Intelligence, 1, 389–399. https://doi.org/10.1038/s42256-019-0088-2
3. Humphreys, P. (2009). *The philosophical novelty of computer simulation methods*. Synthese, 169, 615–626. https://doi.org/10.1007/s11229-008-9435-2
4. Burrell, J. (2016). *How the machine 'thinks': Understanding opacity in machine learning algorithms*. Big Data & Society, 3(1). https://doi.org/10.1177/2053951715622512
5. Mittelstadt, B. D., Allo, P., Taddeo, M., Wachter, S., & Floridi, L. (2016). *The ethics of algorithms: Mapping the debate*. Big Data & Society, 3(2). https://doi.org/10.1177/2053951716679679
6. Mitchell, M., Wu, S., Zaldivar, A., Barnes, P., Vasserman, L., Hutchinson, B., Spitzer, E., Raji, I. D., & Gebru, T. (2019). *Model Cards for Model Reporting*. In *Proceedings of the Conference on Fairness, Accountability, and Transparency (FAT* '19)* (pp. 220–229). Association for Computing Machinery, New York, NY, USA. https://doi.org/10.1145/3287560.3287596
7. Asimov, I. (1950). *Run Around*. In *I, Robot* (The Isaac Asimov Collection ed.). Doubleday, New York.
8. Winfield, A. F., Michael, K., Pitt, J., & Evers, V. (2019). *Machine Ethics: The Design and Governance of Ethical AI and Autonomous Systems [Scanning the Issue]*. Proceedings of the IEEE, 107(3), 509–517. https://doi.org/10.1109/JPROC.2019.2900622
9. Moor, J. H. (2006). *The nature, importance, and difficulty of machine ethics*. IEEE Intelligent Systems, 21(4), 18–21.

10. IEEE Global Initiative on Ethics of Autonomous and Intelligent Systems. (2019). Ethically aligned design: A vision for prioritizing human well-being with autonomous and intelligent systems (1st ed.). Institute of Electrical and Electronics Engineers. https://standards.ieee.org/industry-connections/ec/ethically-aligned-design/
11. Binns, R. (2018). *Fairness in Machine Learning: Lessons from Political Philosophy*. In *Proceedings of the 2018 Conference on Fairness, Accountability, and Transparency* (pp. 149–159). https://proceedings.mlr.press/v81/binns18a.html
12. Association for Computing Machinery. (2018). ACM Code of Ethics and Professional Conduct (ISBN 978-1-4503-6626-7; DOI https://doi.org/10.1145/3274591). https://www.acm.org/binaries/content/assets/about/acm-code-of-ethics-booklet.pdf
13. Future of Life Institute: Asilomar AI Principles. https://futureoflife.org/ai-principles/ (2017)
14. OECD. (2021). *OECD Framework for the Classification of AI Systems*. OECD Publishing. https://www.oecd.org/digital/artificial-intelligence/classification-of-ai-systems.pdf
15. World Economic Forum: AI Governance Frameworks for the Future. Davos Annual Report (2023)
16. National Institute of Standards and Technology (NIST). (2023). *AI Risk Management Framework (AI RMF 1.0)*. U.S. Department of Commerce. https://www.nist.gov/itl/ai-risk-management-framework
17. Liang, F., Das, V., Kostyuk, N., & Hussain, M. M. (2022). Constructing a data-driven society: China's social credit system as a state-driven solution for AI governance. *Policy & Internet*, 14(1), 73–93.
18. Creemers, R. (2017). Cyber China: Upgrading propaganda, public opinion work and social management for the twenty-first century. *Journal of Contemporary China*, 26(103), 85–100.
19. European Parliament and Council. (2024). *Regulation (EU) 2024/1689 on laying down harmonised rules on artificial intelligence (AI Act)*. Official Journal of the European Union.
20. International Organization for Standardization. (2023). *ISO/IEC 23894:2023 Artificial Intelligence—Guidance on risk management*. Geneva, Switzerland.
21. Personal Data Protection Commission (PDPC). (2022). *Model AI Governance Framework (Second Edition)*. Singapore Government. https://www.pdpc.gov.sg/Help-and-Resources/2022/01/Model-AI-Governance-Framework
22. Wiener, N. (1950). *The Human Use of Human Beings: Cybernetics and Society*. Houghton Mifflin.
23. Coglianese, C., & Lehr, D. (2017). *Regulating by Robot: Administrative Decision Making in the Machine-Learning Era*. All Faculty Scholarship, 1734. University of Pennsylvania Law School. https://scholarship.law.upenn.edu/faculty_scholarship/1734

Governance, Legal Responsibility, and Post-Compliance Ethics in AI

3

3.1 AI Governance

A municipal government introduces AI-driven facial recognition technology in public spaces to identify individuals with outstanding warrants and deter criminal activity. Preliminary reports suggest a measurable 20% reduction in reported street-level crimes, prompting city officials to cite the deployment as a success in public safety innovation. However, human rights organizations and community stakeholders raise critical concerns. Documented cases of false positives disproportionately affect ethnic minorities, with several incidents involving unwarranted police stops. Critics argue that the system was deployed without transparent public consent mechanisms or sufficient oversight, potentially undermining civil liberties and procedural justice.

This scenario surfaces a profound ethical dilemma rooted in contrasting philosophical principles:

- Utilitarian stance: Endorses the system's continuation, arguing that the net benefits—reduced crime, enhanced deterrence, and efficient law enforcement—justify the harms caused by occasional misidentifications. Public safety, in this view, is a collective good that may warrant limited individual sacrifices.
- Deontological stance: Opposes the deployment, asserting that violating individuals' rights to privacy, due process, and non-discrimination cannot be justified, regardless of aggregate gains. From this perspective, moral actions must uphold inviolable principles, even at the cost of potential utility.

This ethical tension exemplifies the need for regulatory frameworks that balance collective welfare with foundational rights. It further calls for embedding ethical reasoning in the

R. Andrade et al., *Building Ethical and Secure AI*, Synthesis Lectures on Computer Science,
https://doi.org/10.1007/978-3-032-25789-5_3

Table 3.1 Comparative table of moral philosophies applied to AI

Moral philosophy	Core principle	Application in AI context
Utilitarianism	Maximize overall utility and reduce harm for the greatest number	Used in predictive models for social good (e.g., triage, policing, risk scoring), but may overlook minority harm
Deontological ethics	Actions must adhere to moral rules and duties regardless of consequences	Ensures compliance with human rights, transparency, and dignity in AI systems (e.g., right to explanation)
Ethics of care	Emphasizes empathy, relationships, and context over abstract rules	Applied to participatory AI design, inclusion of marginalized groups, and context-sensitive fairness

lifecycle of AI systems to ensure accountability, transparency, and legitimacy. As shown in Table 3.1, different moral philosophies provide distinct foundations for ethical reasoning in AI design. Each framework—utilitarianism, deontological ethics, and ethics of care—offers unique insights into how AI systems can align with values such as social good, rights-based compliance, and relational fairness.

3.2 Conceptual Framework for AI Governance

A conceptual framework for AI governance provides the foundational structure needed to guide the design, development, deployment, and oversight of artificial intelligence systems. Rather than offering a fixed set of rules, this framework serves as a flexible, yet coherent, set of ideas and principles that help stakeholders understand what is at stake when managing AI technologies—and how to respond in a responsible, context-sensitive manner. Governing artificial intelligence involves more than setting technical standards or drafting isolated regulations. It requires attention to several interrelated areas that shape how AI systems are built, evaluated, and used. These areas, or dimensions, help us think systematically about what it means to guide AI in ways that respect both human and societal needs. Four key dimensions are often highlighted in discussions about governance: normative, institutional, technical, and contextual (Fig. 3.1).

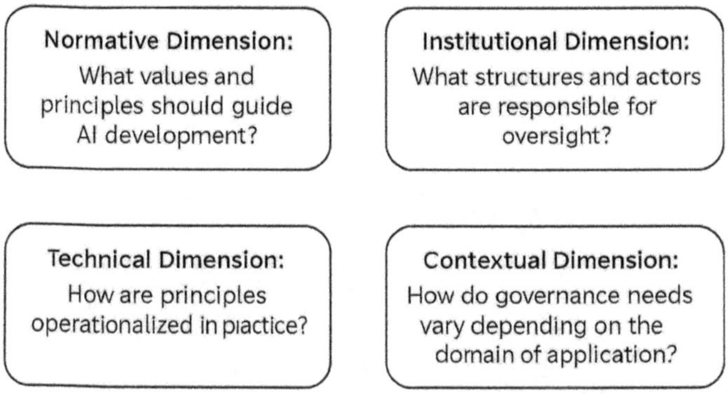

Fig. 3.1 Core dimensions of AI governance

3.2.1 Normative Dimension: What Values and Principles Should Guide the Development of Artificial Intelligence?

Ethical Principles

Imagine an AI system that evaluates credit applications in real time. Its technical accuracy is impressive, yet an analysis reveals that it systematically discriminates against certain socioeconomic groups. This raises the first pillar of ethical governance: fairness and non-discrimination, which demands correcting structural biases and ensuring equitable decisions. But even if the model were fair, how can applicants trust an algorithm they cannot understand? This brings us to transparency and explainability, essential for enabling those affected to comprehend and challenge AI-driven decisions. However, transparency alone is not enough. Who is accountable if a system error causes serious harm? Accountability and responsibility require clear structures for assigning liability, from developers to the institutions deploying the system. All of this must occur without losing sight of human autonomy and dignity: AI should assist, not replace, people's ability to make decisions about their own lives. Finally, the development of these systems must aim for the common good, maximizing benefits while reducing risks, always under strict guarantees of privacy and data protection.

This delicate balance—between technological innovation and human principles—is the true core of AI governance: a constant counterweight that prevents efficiency from displacing justice or innovation from overshadowing dignity. This illustration, Fig. 3.2, symbolizes the ethical imperative of aligning artificial intelligence systems with core human values. It visually reinforces the need for governance frameworks that ensure AI technologies uphold principles such as dignity, autonomy, and justice.

The ethical principles underlying artificial intelligence (AI) governance form the backbone of responsible development, deployment, and oversight of these technologies. AI systems must be designed and implemented with a clear commitment to ethical principles:

Fig. 3.2 Balancing AI and human values

Fairness and Non-discrimination demand that AI systems actively prevent the perpetuation or amplification of societal biases, particularly those affecting historically marginalized or protected groups. In practice, this means scrutinizing training data, refining models, and continuously auditing outputs to ensure equitable treatment.

Transparency and Explainability ensure that AI decision-making processes are interpretable by stakeholders, from technical teams to end users. These principles acknowledge that trust is impossible without understanding: when affected parties can trace how and why decisions are made, accountability becomes tangible, and unjust outcomes can be challenged.

Accountability and Responsibility extend beyond identifying failures; they require clear oversight structures that assign liability throughout the AI system's lifecycle. Developers, organizations, and regulators must share a well-defined duty to anticipate, monitor, and address harms caused by AI applications.

Human Autonomy and Dignity highlight the need to preserve meaningful human control over AI systems. These technologies should augment—not replace—human agency, ensuring that fundamental rights remain protected even in highly automated contexts.

Beneficence and Non-maleficence emphasize maximizing AI's societal benefits while minimizing potential harms. These dual imperatives call for proactive risk assessment and mitigation strategies that prioritize safety and well-being over efficiency alone.

Finally, **Privacy and Data Protection** safeguard personal information through informed consent, stringent data governance, and robust security measures. As AI becomes more pervasive, protecting individual privacy is not optional but essential for sustaining trust in these systems.

Collectively, these principles act as critical anchors for legitimacy in AI governance. They bridge the gap between technological innovation and societal expectations, ensuring that AI serves human values—justice, dignity, autonomy—rather than undermining them.

3.2.2 Institutional Dimension: What Structures and Actors are Responsible for Oversight?

The development and use of artificial intelligence systems must begin with a fundamental question: What values should guide this process? This dimension focuses precisely on that. At its core are rights recognized in law—such as privacy, equal treatment, and human dignity—alongside ethical principles that have become central in contemporary debates, including fairness, responsibility, openness, and the pursuit of collective well-being. A number of international initiatives have helped shape the articulation and institutionalization of these values. The OECD Principles on AI [1], for instance, advocate for a human-centered approach that emphasizes inclusive growth and adherence to legal standards. The Montreal Declaration for Responsible AI [2] underscores the importance of democratic values and individual autonomy in the governance of emerging technologies. The UNESCO Recommendation on the Ethics of Artificial Intelligence [3] expands this ethical landscape by including considerations such as environmental sustainability and social solidarity. Normative dimension includes formal laws and binding regulations such as the EU AI Act [4] or ISO/IEC 23894 [5], which define permissible uses and risk-based classifications of AI systems.

Legal and Regulatory Frameworks: Enforceable Governance Mechanisms

The legal dimension of AI governance plays a pivotal role in establishing binding norms, enforcement mechanisms, and avenues for redress, ensuring that the deployment of AI systems aligns with societal values and legal expectations. Contemporary regulatory frameworks often combine sector-specific mandates with horizontal provisions applicable across domains, thereby addressing both context-sensitive risks and overarching ethical concerns. Central to this legal architecture are instruments such as the European Union's AI Act, which exemplifies a comprehensive legislative approach to AI regulation through a risk-based framework that categorizes systems by their potential harm and imposes proportionate obligations [6]. This model is complemented by amendments to existing legal regimes, such as those governing medical devices or financial services, allowing for the integration of AI-specific safeguards without duplicating normative efforts [7]. Liability regimes further reinforce accountability by delineating responsibilities for harms attributable to autonomous systems, a critical component for legal certainty and victim compensation [8]. Standards and certification schemes—developed by institutions like ISO or IEEE—serve to operationalize abstract principles of safety and robustness into verifiable technical benchmarks [9]. Additionally, procurement policies are increasingly leveraged to promote responsible AI by requiring vendors to comply with ethical and technical requirements as a condition for public sector adoption. Meanwhile, soft-law instruments such as regulatory sandboxes and voluntary codes of conduct offer flexible spaces for innovation under supervised conditions, enabling iterative learning without forgoing oversight [10]. The shift toward risk-based governance represents a nuanced evolution in AI regulation—balancing the imperative for technological progress with the ethical mandate to prevent harm.

Comparative Analysis of Global AI Regulatory Frameworks

The global landscape of AI regulation is characterized by divergent governance models, which reflect varying normative priorities and legal infrastructures. The European Union exemplifies a risk-based approach through its Artificial Intelligence Act (AI Act), which prohibits certain high-risk applications and imposes strict transparency obligations, with fines reaching up to 6% of global annual turnover for non-compliance [4]. This model seeks to safeguard fundamental rights by embedding legal guarantees directly into AI development cycles [11].

In contrast, the United States follows a fragmented sectoral approach, relying heavily on state-level regulations and voluntary federal guidelines such as the AI Bill of Rights. These emphasize fairness and non-discrimination in domains like finance and healthcare, though critics argue this model lacks comprehensive enforceability [12]. Meanwhile, Latin American countries, particularly Brazil and Mexico, are in nascent stages of AI regulation. Their frameworks tend to prioritize economic development and innovation over restrictive compliance, highlighting a trend of techno-economic pragmatism rather than rights-centric governance [6].

This divergence across jurisdictions poses substantial challenges for multinational organizations, leading to legal fragmentation and compliance asymmetries in the global AI marketplace. Scholars advocate for internationally harmonized AI governance principles to reduce regulatory uncertainty and promote ethical consistency across borders [8, 13].

Balancing Innovation and Rights in Contemporary AI Governance

The contemporary paradigm of AI governance must balance the rapid pace of technological innovation with the protection of fundamental rights, especially in an era marked by profound technical and legal uncertainty. This challenge requires what Floridi and Cowls describe as ethical foresight embedded across the AI lifecycle—from design to deployment—ensuring principles such as beneficence, autonomy, justice, and explicability are preserved [11]. Such a holistic approach emphasizes that innovation should not undermine legal guarantees, but rather coexist with them as mutually reinforcing goals.

Early warnings from Wiener about automated systems' societal implications remain strikingly relevant today, underscoring the necessity of integrating human oversight and reliability in AI design [22]. In parallel, regulatory instruments like the EU AI Act attempt to formalize risk-based oversight, promoting both technological growth and human-centric safeguards [4]. Agile governance frameworks further advocate institutional adaptability in response to the evolving nature of AI [6].

By fostering interdisciplinary collaboration and promoting culturally sensitive implementations, governance models can enhance both legitimacy and global adoption. As such, contemporary AI governance must be understood not merely as a regulatory imperative but as a foundational pillar for trustworthy and equitable innovation.

Ultimately, the normative dimension functions as a compass for AI governance. It serves as a reminder that technological design and implementation are never ethically neutral activities—they entail value-laden decisions that reflect particular visions of justice, accountability, and the common good.

3.2.3 Technical Dimension: How are Principles Operationalized in Practice?

Artificial Intelligence (AI) governance refers to the institutionalized set of structures, processes, and mechanisms that guide the development, deployment, and oversight of AI systems. Normative frameworks play a pivotal role in shaping the way AI systems are evaluated and governed. For example, when fairness is a concern, developers must examine how a system's outputs affect different demographic groups. If transparency is prioritized, it becomes necessary to ensure that decisions made by AI systems can be traced and explained through appropriate documentation and interpretability mechanisms.

Technical mechanisms are critical enablers for operationalizing AI governance principles throughout the system lifecycle. These mechanisms translate high-level ethical and legal commitments into practical implementation strategies that span the design, development, and deployment phases. In the design phase, methodologies such as privacy-preserving machine learning (e.g., differential privacy, federated learning) and ethics-by-design practices aim to preemptively mitigate risks by embedding normative considerations early in

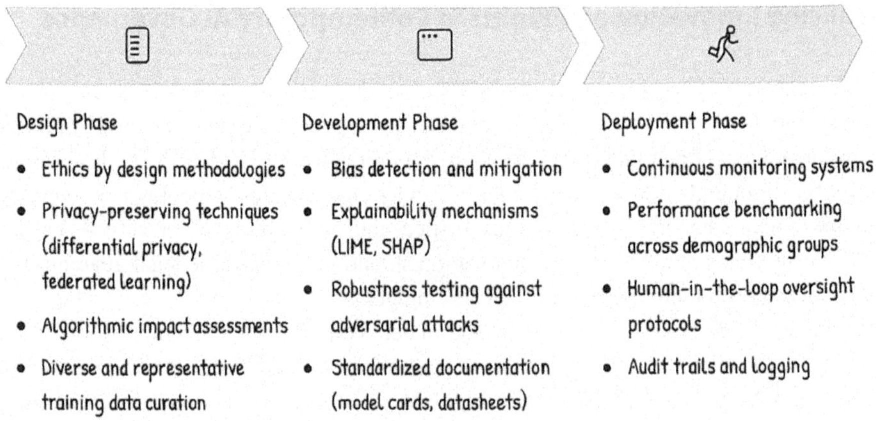

Fig. 3.3 Integrating ethics across the AI system lifecycle

system architecture [11, 15]. During development, the use of bias detection and mitigation tools, explainability frameworks such as LIME and SHAP, and robustness testing against adversarial threats ensures functional reliability and fairness [16, 17]. Furthermore, model documentation tools (e.g., datasheets and model cards) contribute to transparency and traceability [18, 19]. In the deployment phase, governance is reinforced through continuous monitoring, demographic benchmarking, and human-in-the-loop oversight, complemented by audit trails and logging mechanisms to support accountability and legal compliance [20]. Despite these advances, the standardization of technical controls remains a challenge, particularly given the complexity and opacity of modern neural architectures [6]. As such, ongoing efforts by standard-setting bodies and open-source communities are essential for evolving verifiable and interpretable governance solutions.

Figure 3.3 illustrates the integration of ethical principles throughout the AI system lifecycle, from design to deployment.

3.2.4 Contextual Dimension: How Do Governance Needs Vary Depending on the Domain of Application?

Effective governance frameworks emphasize the creation of dedicated oversight bodies, such as AI ethics committees and external advisory boards, which ensure diverse and interdisciplinary perspectives on development and deployment decisions [11]. Cross-functional teams—comprising technical experts, ethicists, legal advisors, and impacted stakeholders—foster collaborative deliberation and holistic risk assessment [6]. These arrangements are supported by clear governance protocols, including documented approval processes, escalation paths, and role-based accountability matrices for monitoring and remediation [21].

Furthermore, training and awareness initiatives play a critical role in equipping all stakeholders with the knowledge of AI ethics and regulatory obligations relevant to their functions [22]. Finally, incentive structures that align ethical behavior with performance evaluations and strategic rewards are essential to encourage responsible innovation across departments [23]. These organizational mechanisms not only institutionalize ethical practices but also operationalize accountability and transparency as core components of trustworthy AI governance.

3.2.4.1 Applied Context: Ethical AI in Practice Across Domains

The *contextual dimension of AI governance* emphasizes that ethical principles must be adapted to the realities of each application domain. The way fairness, transparency, accountability, and privacy are operationalized can differ significantly between healthcare, finance, and human resources. For instance, in **maternal health prediction systems (Pregnancy Risk)**, *beneficence* and *non-maleficence* take precedence, as the aim is to protect lives while ensuring *data privacy* in highly sensitive contexts. In **credit scoring**, *fairness and non-discrimination* become paramount to prevent systemic bias against disadvantaged socioeconomic groups, while *explainability* is crucial for fostering trust among applicants. In **hiring algorithms**, *human dignity and autonomy* require that decisions support, rather than replace, human judgment, with strong oversight mechanisms for accountability. These examples demonstrate that governance principles cannot be applied uniformly; they must be *contextualized*, balancing ethical imperatives with sector-specific risks, regulations, and stakeholder needs.

Table 3.2 illustrates how ethical principles are applied differently across various domains through practical Colab exercises. It highlights that principles such as fairness, transparency, accountability, and privacy are operationalized in distinct ways depending on the context—ranging from safeguarding patient safety in healthcare to ensuring non-discrimination in credit scoring or protecting human dignity in recruitment processes. By mapping each exercise to the core governance dimensions (normative, technical, institutional, and contextual), the table demonstrates that effective AI governance requires a tailored approach that adapts ethical guidelines to the specific risks, stakeholders, and regulatory frameworks of each domain.

3.2.4.2 Global Coordination in AI Governance

Global coordination in AI governance has become imperative as artificial intelligence systems increasingly impact transnational data flows, algorithmic accountability, and international supply chains. Several multilateral efforts exemplify this shift toward collaborative norm-setting. The OECD AI Principles, endorsed by over 40 countries, provide a foundational policy framework emphasizing human-centered values, transparency, and accountability. Similarly, the UNESCO Recommendation on AI Ethics stands as the first universally negotiated normative instrument on AI, offering guidance on sustainability, data gover-

Table 3.2 Comparative table: ethical principles, and governance dimensions

Domain	Key ethical principles	Governance dimensions involved
Pregnancy risk prediction (Healthcare)	Beneficence, Non-maleficence, Privacy, Accountability	Normative (ethical imperatives for patient safety), Technical (privacy-preserving modeling), Contextual (adaptation to healthcare regulation)
Healthcare outcomes prediction	Privacy, Transparency, Fairness	Normative (data protection and equity), Technical (model interpretability tools such as SHAP), Contextual (alignment with health data standards)
Credit scoring fairness (Finance)	Fairness, Non-discrimination, Transparency	Normative (justice in financial decisions), Technical (bias detection and mitigation methods), Institutional (oversight for credit decision processes)
Recruitment algorithms (Human resources)	Human dignity, Autonomy, Accountability, Fairness	Normative (respect for individual rights), Institutional (clear accountability frameworks in hiring), Contextual (adapting governance to HR practices and labor law)

nance, and equity—especially for developing nations. In parallel, the Global Partnership on AI (GPAI) advances responsible AI through multi-stakeholder research, focusing on challenges such as data governance and the impact of pandemics. Standard-setting bodies like ISO/IEC JTC 1/SC 42 and the IEEE Global Initiative on Ethics of Autonomous and Intelligent Systems contribute by developing technical specifications for risk, bias mitigation, and ethical compliance. Despite these efforts, significant obstacles persist: divergent regulatory traditions, geopolitical tensions, and stark capacity gaps between the Global North and South hinder harmonization. Future progress depends on creating interoperable standards that balance universal ethical commitments with regional contextualization, supported by robust enforcement and monitoring infrastructures.

The increasing adoption of artificial intelligence in critical infrastructures has prompted the development of dedicated security standards and governance frameworks to address unique risks posed by AI systems. Notably, the NIST AI Risk Management Framework provides a structured approach for categorizing, measuring, and mitigating AI risks, emphasizing governance and institutional accountability in both public and private sectors. Concurrently, the ISO/IEC 42001—currently under development—aims to standardize security controls within AI management systems, laying the groundwork for global interoperability and assurance.

Table 3.3 Comparative AI regulatory approaches by jurisdiction

Jurisdiction	Approach	Key features
European Union	Comprehensive regulation with tiered risk categories	Prohibited applications, conformity assessments for high-risk systems, transparency requirements
United States	Sector-specific regulation with voluntary standards	FTC enforcement, NIST risk-management framework, state-level legislation
China	Algorithm-focused regulation with security emphasis	Classification systems, data controls, content restrictions
United Kingdom	Pro-innovation approach with sectoral oversight	Regulatory principles, sector regulator coordination, standards development

As shown in Table 3.3, regulatory strategies for AI differ significantly between the European Union, United States, China, and the United Kingdom, reflecting contrasting priorities such as security, innovation, and sectoral oversight.

The OWASP Top 10 for LLM Applications reflects a more agile, community-driven initiative, highlighting prevalent vulnerabilities in large language models and offering targeted mitigation strategies. From a regulatory perspective, the EU AI Act Security Requirements represent a risk-based legislative approach mandating compliance mechanisms by 2025, thereby operationalizing ethical and safety principles into enforceable legal norms. Collectively, these initiatives reflect a convergence of technical, organizational, and regulatory efforts, reinforcing the need for multi-layered and adaptive security postures in AI governance frameworks [24–27]. Table 3.4 summarizes key AI security standards and frameworks, outlining their organizational origins, coverage areas, and current implementation status.

Table 3.4 Key AI security standards and frameworks

Standard/Framework	Organization	Coverage areas	Implementation status
AI risk-management framework	NIST	Governance, measurement, categorization	Released 1.0, adoption growing
ISO/IEC 42001	ISO	AI management systems, security controls	Draft stage, expected 2024
OWASP top 10 for LLM Applications	OWASP	Common vulnerabilities, mitigation guidance	Active, regularly updated
EU AI act security requirements	European union	Risk-based security requirements	Approved, compliance required by 2025

Intervention in the AI lifecycle

- At which stages (design, training, deployment) should ethics committees intervene?
- How can citizen participation be incorporated into these stages?

3.3 Key Takeaways

1. **AI Governance Requires Multidimensional Approaches**: Effective governance of AI systems demands integration across *normative, institutional, technical, and contextual dimensions*, ensuring that ethical principles are translated into actionable oversight mechanisms.
2. **Legal Compliance is a Baseline, Not the Goal**: Regulatory frameworks such as the *EU AI Act* provide essential guardrails, but *post-compliance ethics*—including transparency, fairness, and explainability—are critical to maintaining public trust and preventing societal harm.
3. **Ethical Principles Must Be Technically Operationalized**: Concepts such as *accountability*, *non-maleficence*, and *autonomy* must be embedded in AI through *bias mitigation*, *explainable AI (XAI)*, *impact assessments*, and *documentation artifacts* (e.g., model cards and datasheets).
4. **Institutional Accountability is Essential**: Governance structures must include *ethics committees, legal oversight bodies, and stakeholder participation* to align AI development with *human-centered values* and democratic norms.
5. **Global Coordination and Local Adaptation Must Coexist**: While international standards promote coherence, *context-sensitive governance* is crucial to address the sociotechnical realities of diverse regions and vulnerable populations.

Chapter 4 will focus on the role of security as a verifiable ethical imperative in AI, including threat modeling and resilience against adversarial attacks.

References

1. OECD. (2021). *OECD Framework for the Classification of AI Systems*. OECD Publishing. https://www.oecd.org/digital/artificial-intelligence/classification-of-ai-systems.pdf
2. Universite de Montreal. (2018). Montreal Declaration for a Responsible Development of Artificial Intelligence. Retrieved from https://www.montrealdeclaration-responsibleai.com/
3. UNESCO. (2021). *Recommendation on the Ethics of Artificial Intelligence*. United Nations Educational, Scientific and Cultural Organization. Retrieved from https://unesdoc.unesco.org/ark:/48223/pf0000381137
4. European Union. *Artificial Intelligence Act*. Disponible en: https://artificialintelligenceact.eu/the-act/. Consultado el 23 de julio de 2025.

5. ISO/IEC. *Information technology – Artificial intelligence – Guidance on risk management (ISO/IEC 23894:2023)*. Publicada en febrero de 2023. Disponible en: https://www.iso.org/standard/77304.html. Consultado el 23 de julio de 2025.
6. D. Kumar, K. Kumar, R. K. Choudhary and V. Singh, "Cultural Intelligence in AI Ethics: A Systematic Framework for Implementation Across Global Contexts," 2025 3rd International Conference on Intelligent Systems, Advanced Computing and Communication (ISACC), Silchar, India, 2025, pp. 538-545, https://doi.org/10.1109/ISACC65211.2025.10969295.
7. Agarwal, A., & Nene, M.J. (2025). *A five-layer framework for AI governance: Integrating regulation, standards, and certification*. Transforming Government: People, Process and Policy.
8. Ricciardi Celsi, L., & Zomaya, A. Y. (2025). Perspectives on Managing AI Ethics in the Digital Age. Information, 16(4), 318. https://doi.org/10.3390/info16040318
9. Shi, J., Wang, G., & Wang, Y. (2024). *Artificial intelligence foundation model risk identification and governance model from the ESG perspective*. Bulletin of Chinese Academy of Sciences.
10. Kattnig, M., Angerschmid, A., Reichel, T., & Kern, R. (2024). Assessing trustworthy AI: Technical and legal perspectives of fairness in AI. Computer Law & Security Review, 55, 106053. https://doi.org/10.1016/j.clsr.2024.106053
11. Floridi, L., & Cowls, J. (2019). *A Unified Framework of Five Principles for AI in Society*. Harvard Data Science Review, 1(1). https://doi.org/10.1162/99608f92.8cd550d1
12. Lehr, D., & Ohm, P. (2017). *Playing with the Data: What Legal Scholars Should Learn about Machine Learning*. UC Davis Law Review, 51(2), 653–717.
13. Atoum, I. (2025). *Revolutionizing AI Governance: Addressing Bias and Ensuring Accountability Through the Holistic AI Governance Framework*. International Journal of Advanced Computer Science and Applications.
14. Amann, J., Blasimme, A., Vayena, E., Frey, D., & Madai, V. I. (2020). *Explainability for artificial intelligence in healthcare: A multidisciplinary perspective*. BMC Medical Informatics and Decision Making, 20(1), 310. BioMed Central. Retrieved from https://doi.org/10.1186/s12911-020-01332-6
15. Dwork, C., & Ilvento, C. (2018). Fairness under composition (arXiv:1806.06122). arXiv. https://doi.org/10.48550/arXiv.1806.06122
16. Ribeiro, M. T., Singh, S., & Guestrin, C. (2016). "Why should I trust you?": Explaining the predictions of any classifier. In *Proceedings of the 22nd ACM SIGKDD International Conference on Knowledge Discovery and Data Mining* (pp. 1135–1144).
17. Shapley, L. S. (1953). A value for n-person games. In H. W. Kuhn & A. W. Tucker (Eds.), *Contributions to the Theory of Games II* (pp. 307–317). Princeton University Press.
18. Gebru, T., Morgenstern, J., Vecchione, B., Vaughan, J. W., Wallach, H., Daumé III, H., & Crawford, K. (2018). Datasheets for datasets. *arXiv preprint* arXiv:1803.09010.
19. Mitchell, M., Wu, S., Zaldivar, A., Barnes, P., Vasserman, L., Hutchinson, B., Spitzer, E., Raji, I. D., & Gebru, T. (2019). Model cards for model reporting. En Proceedings of the 2019 Conference on Fairness, Accountability, and Transparency (FAT '19)* (pp. 220–229). Association for Computing Machinery. https://doi.org/10.1145/3287560.3287596
20. Brundage, M., Avin, S., Wang, J., Belfield, H., Krueger, G., Hadfield, G., Khlaaf, H., Yang, J., Toner, H., Fong, R., Maharaj, T., Koh, P. W., Hooker, S., Leung, J., Trask, A., Bluemke, E., Lebensold, J., O'Keefe, C., Koren, M., ... Anderljung, M. (2020). Toward trustworthy AI development: Mechanisms for supporting verifiable claims (arXiv:2004.07213). arXiv. https://doi.org/10.48550/arXiv.2004.07213
21. Jobin, A., Ienca, M., & Vayena, E. (2019). *The global landscape of AI ethics guidelines*. Nature Machine Intelligence, 1, 389–399. https://doi.org/10.1038/s42256-019-0088-2
22. Morley, J., Floridi, L., Kinsey, L., & Elhalal, A. (2021). *From what to how: An initial review of publicly available AI ethics tools, methods and research to translate principles into practices*. Science and Engineering Ethics, 27(1), 1–31.

23. Kandeel, M. E., Hamza, E. A., & Elrefae, G. (2024). AI governance: A general perspective. En Global Congress on Emerging Technologies, GCET 2024 (pp. 195–201). Institute of Electrical and Electronics Engineers Inc. https://doi.org/10.1109/GCET64327.2024.10934585
24. National Institute of Standards and Technology. (2023). *AI Risk Management Framework 1.0*. U.S. Department of Commerce.
25. International Organization for Standardization. (2023). *ISO/IEC 42001 - AI Management System Standard (Draft)*.
26. OWASP Foundation. (2024). *OWASP Top 10 for Large Language Model Applications*. https://owasp.org/www-project-top-10-for-llm/
27. European Commission. (2023). *Proposal for a Regulation on Artificial Intelligence (AI Act)*. Brussels: European Union.

Bias and Fairness in Applied AI Systems 4

4.1 The Critical Role of Explainability and Fairness in High-Stakes AI Systems

Imagine an AI system predicting pregnancy risks, prioritizing access to healthcare, evaluating credit applications, or ranking candidates for a job. These are not hypothetical scenarios, each exposing how algorithms can unintentionally reproduce and amplify structural inequalities. In the pregnancy risk prediction model, fairness means ensuring that expectant mothers from marginalized backgrounds are not overclassified as "high risk" due to biased historical data, while explainability allows patients and clinicians to understand why certain health factors drive these classifications. In healthcare access modeling, fairness safeguards equitable prioritization of patients across socioeconomic and demographic groups, and explainability transforms opaque decisions into transparent, justifiable pathways that can be challenged when they appear unjust. In credit scoring, fairness protects against discriminatory practices that deny loans based on proxies like ZIP codes, while explainability provides applicants with understandable reasons for approval or rejection—critical for building trust and complying with fair lending regulations. In recruitment systems, fairness ensures that candidates are evaluated on merit rather than gender, age, or educational background, and explainability gives applicants and organizations visibility into the factors influencing rankings, enabling contestation of biased outcomes. These cases illustrate why fairness and explainability are not optional features but essential pillars for building AI systems that are socially just, trustworthy, and accountable.

Judicial AI Systems: COMPAS and Algorithmic Bias

One of the most high-profile controversies in algorithmic fairness is the COMPAS tool used in the U.S. justice system to assess recidivism risk. According to a ProPublica investigation, the tool exhibited racial bias: Black defendants were nearly twice as likely as white

R. Andrade et al., *Building Ethical and Secure AI*, Synthesis Lectures on Computer Science,
https://doi.org/10.1007/978-3-032-25789-5_4

defendants to be incorrectly labeled as high risk [1]. This raised concerns about disparate false positive rates, opacity in decision-making, and the use of biased historical data, which perpetuated systemic inequalities. Scholars such as Barocas et al. [2] emphasize that such tools lack fairness constraints and fail to uphold due process, prompting calls for the integration of fairness-aware metrics and pre-deployment audits.

Hiring Platforms: Gender Bias in Resume Screening

Amazon discontinued its AI-based hiring tool after discovering gender discrimination in its outputs. Trained on 10 years of resumes submitted mostly by male candidates, the model learned to penalize resumes containing words like "women's chess club" or graduates from women's colleges [3]. The case illustrated how historical bias and proxy variables can lead to discriminatory predictions. In response, modern hiring platforms are adopting fairness-aware preprocessing, adversarial debiasing, and audit frameworks such as IBM's AI Fairness 360 Toolkit and Microsoft's Fairlearn.

Financial Scoring: Fair Lending and Regulatory Compliance

AI models used in credit risk assessment must comply with regulatory frameworks such as the Equal Credit Opportunity Act (ECOA) in the U.S., which prohibits discrimination based on race, gender, or marital status. Despite this, research shows that models often learn discriminatory patterns from proxies like zip codes or transaction histories [4]. To mitigate this, financial institutions use disparate impact analysis, reject inference techniques, and counterfactual fairness testing [5]. These methods ensure that decisions are equitable and comply with legal obligations.

Bias and fairness in applied AI are particularly critical in socially impactful domains where algorithmic decisions have real consequences on individuals and communities. In the justice system, tools like COMPAS have demonstrated how biased risk assessments can disproportionately affect minority defendants, undermining the principle of equal treatment before the law. In employment, AI-driven hiring platforms have historically favored male candidates due to training data reflecting gender imbalances, thereby reproducing occupational segregation. In the financial sector, credit scoring algorithms have denied access to loans or increased interest rates for marginalized groups, often based on proxy variables like ZIP codes or income history. These cases underscore that bias in AI is not a technical inconvenience—it is a social and ethical threat that can institutionalize discrimination at scale. Ensuring fairness in such systems is therefore essential not just for compliance, but for protecting civil rights and fostering trust in automated technologies.

4.2 Digital Platforms: Beliefs and Misinformation

Digital platforms such as Facebook, YouTube, and X (formerly Twitter) utilize algorithmic recommendation systems that personalize content delivery in response to individual user behaviors, preferences, and patterns of interaction [6]. While the goal is to enhance user engagement, these algorithms can inadvertently:

- Create echo chambers by continuously reinforcing a user's pre-existing beliefs, these systems contribute to the formation of digital echo chambers [7].
- Amplify misinformation by favoring emotionally charged or sensationalist content that garners more clicks [8].
- Polarize political discourse, by promoting ideologically extreme viewpoints and suppressing moderate or opposing voices [8].

The algorithms do not inherently understand the impact of what they recommend. They optimize for metrics like click-through rates or watch time, not truthfulness or societal harmony. While the influence of AI on social media platforms—such as content recommendation, political polarization, and misinformation—has received widespread attention, it is important to recognize that there are other social contexts where the impact of algorithmic bias can be even more severe and immediate.

4.3 Social and Technical Dimensions of Algorithmic Bias

Bias in artificial intelligence systems must be examined through both a technical and a social lens to fully grasp its complexity and consequences:

Technically, bias can emerge from unbalanced datasets, flawed feature selection, or inadequate evaluation metrics [9], often leading to reduced performance for underrepresented groups [10]. Engineers typically address these issues using tools such as data augmentation, re-weighting strategies, or fairness-aware algorithms [11]. However, these solutions, while necessary, are not sufficient. Recent research has highlighted how feature-wise interactions can amplify underlying biases in data [12], and how directional biases in model predictions may emerge even in seemingly neutral models [13]. Moreover, generative adversarial approaches have been proposed as advanced methods to actively mitigate such structural inequities [14], further underscoring that fairness in AI systems must be pursued beyond superficial adjustments.

Socially, bias is intertwined with historical inequalities and systemic discrimination reflected in the data itself. For example, a facial recognition model may underperform on darker skin tones not due to a mere lack of data, but because of longstanding societal neglect and exclusion [15–17]. Addressing such bias requires more than algorithmic fairness; it demands critical reflection on power structures, participatory design with marginalized communities, and institutional accountability [18, 19]. Therefore, understanding and mitigating bias in AI is not only a matter of technical correctness but also a profound ethical responsibility [20, 21].

Algorithmic bias can emerge at any stage in the machine learning lifecycle—from data collection and model training to deployment and evaluation. Understanding algorithmic bias, therefore, requires analyzing not only how algorithms compute, but also what values and assumptions they silently embed. It is here that ethical scrutiny, inclusive design, and interdisciplinary collaboration become essential in preventing harm and promoting social justice in the deployment of AI systems. Algorithmic bias manifests in various forms, each rooted in distinct stages of data processing and collection. As commonly identified in the literature, five primary types of bias illustrate the multifaceted nature of this problem:

- Human biases—such as visual perception errors or cognitive shortcuts—often propagate into AI systems. Examples include facial recognition models that perform worse on certain demographics due to unbalanced training data [15, 16].
- Label bias: Bias introduced by errors or inconsistencies in how data is annotated. Annotators' demographic backgrounds influence how they label images or text (e.g., subjective emotion labeling in datasets) [22].
- Sampling bias: Underrepresentation of certain groups or regions in the dataset. Facial recognition systems trained mostly on lighter-skinned faces perform worse on darker-skinned individuals [23].
- Measurement bias: Systematic errors in data collection instruments. Retrospective clinical studies often suffer from recall bias, distorting associations between exposure and outcome [24].
- Historical bias : Bias inherited from structural inequalities embedded in historical data. Credit scoring models penalize minority groups due to discriminatory past financial practices [25].

This dual perspective—technical and social—naturally leads to the broader concept of *algorithmic bias*, which encapsulates how automated decision-making systems can systematically favor certain groups over others. Algorithmic bias arises when patterns of inequality embedded in the training data, combined with optimization objectives that prioritize accuracy or engagement over fairness, result in outputs that reinforce existing disparities [9, 10]. Importantly, such bias is not always the result of malicious intent, rather, it often emerges from opaque design choices, incomplete datasets, or the uncritical reuse of historical information [12, 13]. For instance, in predictive hiring tools or credit scoring systems, models trained on past decisions may unintentionally replicate gender or racial biases that were never explicitly encoded but are statistically present [11].

4.4 Techniques to Address Bias

In a world where machine learning systems increasingly influence decisions about access to healthcare, employment, education, and credit, ensuring ethical safeguards is not a luxury—it is a necessity. As these systems shape human outcomes at scale, they must be held to standards that reflect our shared values of justice, transparency, and responsibility. A fair IA system integrates ethical safeguards into every stage of the machine learning pipeline. The following components are essential to mitigate bias and promote trustworthy AI:

- **Equal Treatment Across Demographic Groups** The system should ensure that outcomes are consistent across protected groups such as race, gender, age, and socioeconomic status. Techniques such as *demographic parity*, *equal opportunity*, and *disparate impact analysis* can be used to evaluate this dimension [26, 27].
- **Transparency in Decision-Making** Transparency involves model interpretability (e.g., LIME, SHAP), open documentation of data sources and modeling choices, and accessible explanations for stakeholders. It enables external audits and empowers affected individuals to contest outcomes [28–30].
- **Accountability for Outcomes** Accountability mechanisms should include audit logs, clear role definitions, and processes for investigating and remedying harms. This aligns with ethical AI governance and supports legal compliance [31, 32].

Equal Treatment Across Demographic Groups
AI systems operating in high-stakes domains such as healthcare must be held to standards of distributive justice, especially when their decisions can directly impact access to essential services. In the Healthcare Access Prediction and Pregnancy Risk Classification scenarios, models risk perpetuating structural inequities by reflecting patterns of historical discrimination embedded in the data. Without intentional safeguards, algorithms may replicate or even exacerbate disparities—systematically deprioritizing individuals from marginalized racial groups, lower socioeconomic strata, or specific gender identities. To counteract these risks, such systems must be conceptualized not as neutral computational tools, but as normatively charged socio-technical instruments. This perspective aligns with the view of AI as embedded in social contexts, as articulated in frameworks like Fairness, Accountability, and Transparency in Machine Learning (FATML) and echoed in global AI governance efforts. Practically, this necessitates fairness-aware preprocessing strategies such as rebalancing datasets, removing or mitigating proxy variables, and feature selection audits to prevent indirect discrimination.

Moreover, evaluation metrics like demographic parity, equalized odds, or disparate impact analysis serve as quantitative means to assess and validate group-level fairness. These metrics do not merely fulfill regulatory checkboxes; they help operationalize the ethical commitment to treat individuals equitably, regardless of identity markers that have historically mediated access to healthcare. When coupled with community-informed validation processes, they ensure that models are both mathematically fair and socially legitimate. Ensuring equal treatment across demographic groups is not only a technical challenge but a moral obligation.

Transparency in Decision-Making

In the case of transparency, in the Healthcare Access Prediction context, transparency means more than technical openness; it means ensuring that a patient denied priority care can understand whether the system made that decision based on clinical need or embedded socioeconomic bias. Using tools like LIME, health professionals can visualize how specific features—such as income level, age, or geographic location—contributed to a risk assessment, allowing for critical evaluation and ethical oversight.

In Pregnancy Risk Classification, transparency helps ensure that automated classifications do not reinforce outdated paternalistic practices. By clearly exposing how risk levels are determined—especially if they influence prenatal interventions or medical advice—pregnant individuals and care providers gain agency to challenge decisions that may not align with personal or contextual realities. For instance, a system that flags young, unmarried women as "high risk" based on biased historical data would be unjustifiable unless transparent reasoning and contestability mechanisms are built in.

In Personnel Selection, transparency counters the black-box nature of many recruitment tools. Job candidates deserve to know whether their age, gender, or educational background affected their ranking. By incorporating SHAP-based explanations and offering feedback portals, organizations can move toward hiring practices that are not only fair but accountable—allowing rejected candidates to see why and request reviews when bias is suspected.

In the case of Credit Allocation Equity, transparency transforms access to finance from a mysterious verdict to a justified evaluation. A system that declines a microloan should explain whether repayment history, debt ratio, or a discriminatory proxy such as neighborhood influenced the outcome. With interpretable models and documented decision rules, institutions can foster trust, reduce exclusion, and comply with regulatory scrutiny.

Accountability for Outcomes

Accountability in AI is the ethical anchor that transforms algorithms from inscrutable machinery into systems answerable to human consequences. In the Healthcare Access Prediction scenario, accountability begins with maintaining detailed audit logs that trace every decision made by the model—from the preprocessing stage to the final prioritization of care. If a patient from a low-income area is persistently deprioritized, these records offer a transparent trail to investigate whether systemic bias influenced access, enabling healthcare administrators to intervene and remedy harm.

In Pregnancy Risk Classification, accountability mechanisms ensure that predictions influencing medical guidance are not accepted as infallible. By defining clear roles—such as distinguishing between the data scientist's responsibility for model design and the clinician's for final judgment—health systems can avoid the abdication of decision-making to algorithms. Additionally, when pregnant individuals face restrictive interventions based on AI outputs, processes must exist to contest and correct unjust or non-contextual outcomes, especially when those outcomes intersect with issues of gender, autonomy, and reproductive rights.

In the Personnel Selection, accountability is essential to protect labor rights. Organizations must document how decisions were made, by whom, and under what criteria—particularly when rejecting applicants. When candidates raise concerns about discrimination, internal auditing mechanisms and external appeals channels must allow for timely review and resolution, affirming the right to due process. This is critical not only for fairness but also for legal compliance with non-discrimination and equal opportunity employment laws.

Finally, in the Credit Allocation Equity context, financial institutions have a duty to explain why a loan was denied—and to whom that explanation is owed. Accountability entails not only transparent reasoning (e.g., feature impact via SHAP) but also the institutional responsibility to investigate disparities in approval rates across regions, gender, and income groups. When audit logs reveal recurring denials to historically excluded communities, remediation plans—such as retraining models or revising lending policies—become ethical imperatives.

Together, these accountability measures convert AI systems from passive calculators into active participants in a governance framework. They ensure that when harm occurs, someone is not only responsible—but empowered to make it right.

4.5 Explainable Artificial Intelligence (XAI)

Explainable Artificial Intelligence (XAI) refers to a set of methods and principles aimed at making the decision-making processes of AI systems—especially complex models such as deep neural networks—understandable to humans. The goal of XAI is to enhance trust, transparency, and accountability by providing insights into how and why a model reaches a particular prediction [33].

Figure 4.1 illustrates the concept of Explainable Artificial Intelligence (XAI) by contrasting a traditional "black-box" AI system with an explainable approach. Initially, an external input—an image of an apple—is processed by a mystery box, which outputs a decision: "It's an apple!" However, the reasoning behind this output remains hidden. XAI intervenes by opening the black box and revealing the underlying rationale, such as recognizing the object as an apple due to its shape and color. This visualization highlights the importance of transparency and interpretability in AI systems, especially in contexts where understanding the basis of decisions is critical for trust, accountability, and ethical deployment.

Fig. 4.1 Contrasting black-box algorithms versus XAI

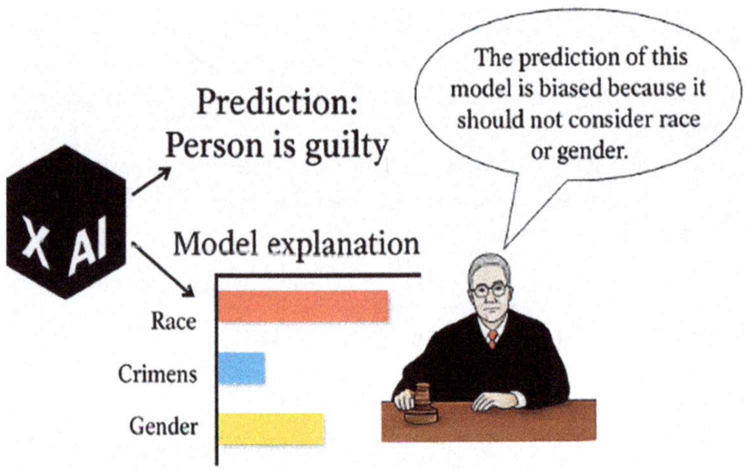

Fig. 4.2 Possible race bias in the model of guilty prediction

Explainability is critical in high-stakes applications such as healthcare, finance, and criminal justice, where decisions must be traceable and justifiable. Figure 4.2 illustrates how Explainable AI (XAI) can reveal potential biases in automated decision-making systems. An input to a black-box model labeled "XAI," which generates a prediction stating that the person is guilty. Alongside this prediction, the system provides an explanation showing that race and gender heavily influenced the outcome. Such a model is biased, as it relies on attributes like race and gender that should not be considered in fair decision-making.

Applied Ethical Dilemmas in AI Systems

Facial Recognition and Surveillance

- What are the ethical limits of using this technology by governments?
- Should it be banned in contexts like schools or protests?

AI in Healthcare

- How can we balance the benefits of accurate diagnostics with patient privacy?
- Should patients have the right to refuse automated diagnoses?

Bias in Automated Recruitment

- How can biases in AI hiring systems be detected and mitigated?
- Should the use of AI for employee recruitment be banned?

AI in Judicial Systems

- Is it ethical for judges to use algorithms to determine sentences?
- How can we ensure AI does not perpetuate historical biases in the justice system?

4.5.1 Key Components of XAI

Understanding the effectiveness of Explainable Artificial Intelligence (XAI) requires examining its foundational dimensions, which go beyond technical transparency to address the human intelligibility of algorithmic decisions. XAI includes the following concepts such as

- **Transparency:** Understanding the internal structure and mechanisms of the model.
- **Interpretability:** The degree to which a human can understand the cause of a decision.
- **Justifiability:** Whether the explanation aligns with social, ethical, or legal expectations.
- **Fidelity:** How accurately the explanation reflects the true behavior of the model.
- **Local versus Global Explanations:** Local explanations refer to individual predictions, while global explanations describe the overall behavior of the model.

XAI involves both technical and human-centered dimensions. On the technical side, it includes methods for revealing the influence of input features, visualizing attention mechanisms, or approximating black-box behavior with interpretable models [30]. On the human side, it concerns the comprehensibility of explanations, their relevance to the audience, and their consistency with ethical and legal standards [29]. Common XAI techniques include LIME, SHAP, counterfactual explanations, saliency maps, and feature importance plots.

The integration of explainability frameworks such as LIME (Local Interpretable Model-agnostic Explanations) and SHAP (SHapley Additive exPlanations) plays a critical role in the auditing and debugging of machine learning models, especially in high-stakes applications involving fairness and accountability. These tools help uncover the underlying logic of a model's decisions by approximating the contribution of each feature to a given prediction, either locally (for individual instances) or globally (across the model). Through this lens, stakeholders can identify potential sources of bias, detect reliance on spurious correlations, and evaluate whether sensitive attributes directly or indirectly influence outcomes. Moreover, explainability enables domain experts and auditors to challenge and validate the model's behavior, promoting transparency and trust. Importantly, while these tools provide insights into black-box systems, they should be used in conjunction with fairness metrics and bias detection frameworks to provide a more complete picture of model reliability and ethical alignment. Auditing practices based on these techniques also support regulatory compliance and can inform necessary interventions, such as feature suppression, retraining, or policy adjustments (Table 4.1).

Figure 4.3 demonstrates the practical application of explainable artificial intelligence (XAI) by visualizing the decision-making process of a medical prediction model. Through a combination of predicted probabilities, a rule-based decision pathway, and feature-specific input values, the model provides transparency into how the diagnosis of diabetes was reached.

Table 4.1 Comparison of SHAP and LIME on key interpretability metrics

Metrics	SHAP	LIME
Concept	Applies to the model as-is	Fits a local surrogate model to explain the complex model
Theory	Additive feature attribution based on game theory	Feature perturbation method
Type	Post hoc model-agnostic	Post hoc model-agnostic
Data type	Images, tabular data, and signals	Images, tabular data, and signals
Explanation	Global, local	Local
Collinearity consideration	Not in the original method	No
Non-linear decision	Depends on the used model	Incapable
Computing time	Higher	Lower
Visualization	Waterfall, Beeswarm, and Summary plots	One single plot

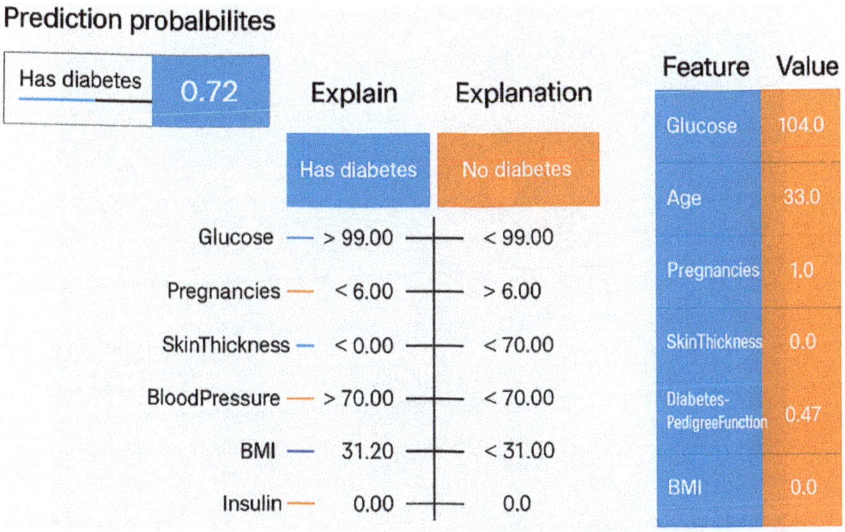

Fig. 4.3 Explainable AI on medical prediction model

By exposing the influence of individual variables, such as glucose levels, age, and number of pregnancies, the graphic supports interpretability and accountability—key principles in trustworthy AI systems.

Machine learning models such as decision trees or linear regressions are generally easier to interpret, offering transparency and straightforward explanations. However, their predictive power tends to be limited, especially in complex or high-dimensional tasks. In contrast, advanced AI models—such as deep neural networks and large language models—have achieved predictive capabilities comparable to or even surpassing human performance in certain domains. Yet, this increase in accuracy comes at the cost of explainability, as their internal workings are often opaque and difficult to interpret, raising challenges for accountability and trust (Fig. 4.4).

4.5.1.1 LIME: Local Interpretable Model-Agnostic Explanations

Local Interpretable Model-agnostic Explanations (LIME) is a widely adopted technique in the field of Explainable Artificial Intelligence (XAI), valued for its accessibility and simplicity. The name itself reflects its core principles: *model-agnosticism* refers to LIME's ability to explain the predictions of any supervised learning model—regardless of its internal structure—by treating it as a black-box function. This makes LIME compatible with a wide range of classifiers and regressors, including deep learning models. Meanwhile, the term *local* emphasizes that LIME generates explanations that are faithful to the model's behavior in the immediate neighborhood of a specific instance, rather than globally approximating the entire decision surface.

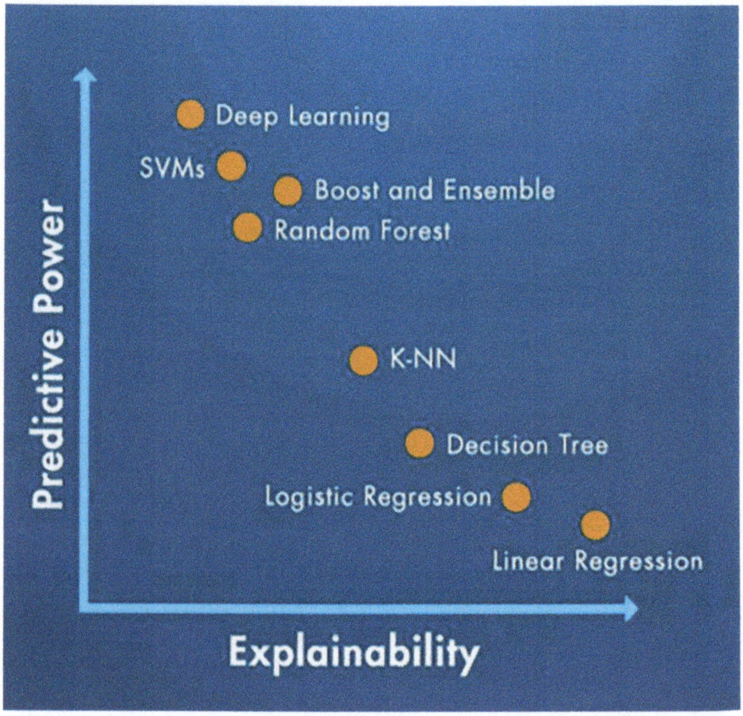

Fig. 4.4 The impact of Explainability over algorithms

Although LIME is currently limited to supervised machine learning and deep learning applications, it remains one of the most widely used and cited XAI methods. Its open-source implementation is available in both R and Python, and its GitHub repository[1] has received significant community engagement, with over 8,000 stars and 2,000 forks.

When provided with a trained predictive model and a test instance, LIME follows a three-step process:

1. **Sampling and Surrogate Dataset Generation:** LIME generates a set of perturbed samples around the instance to be explained—typically 5,000 samples by default. These samples are drawn from a normal distribution centered on the original instance. The black-box model is then used to predict outcomes for these new samples.
2. **Proximity Weighting:** Each perturbed sample is weighted based on its proximity to the original instance, usually using an exponential kernel. This ensures that samples closer to the instance have a stronger influence on the explanation.
3. **Feature Selection and Surrogate Modeling:** LIME applies a feature selection technique, such as Lasso (L1-regularized regression), to identify the most influential fea-

[1] https://github.com/marcotcr/lime.

tures. It then fits a simple, interpretable surrogate model—such as linear regression—on the weighted samples. This surrogate model approximates the behavior of the complex model locally.

By analyzing the coefficients of the surrogate model, LIME highlights which input features contributed most to the original prediction, offering users a transparent, instance-level explanation of the model's decision.

4.5.1.2 SHAP for Feature Attribution and Model Interpretation

SHAP (SHapley Additive exPlanations) is a post hoc, model-agnostic method that can be applied to any machine learning model to quantify feature importance. Based on game theory, SHAP attributes the overall model output to individual input features by treating them as "players" in a cooperative game whose "payout" is the model prediction. The SHAP value of a feature represents its average marginal contribution across all possible combinations (coalitions) of features. Due to the exponential computational cost associated with computing exact Shapley values, particularly as the number of features increases, an approximation called *Kernel SHAP* has been developed.

SHAP has been widely adopted across various domains to generate both local and global explanations of model behavior. However, one critical aspect for practitioners to consider is its model-dependent nature: the importance ranking of features produced by SHAP can vary across different models trained on the same dataset. To demonstrate this, we applied four classifiers—Decision Tree (DT), Logistic Regression (LR), LightGBM (LGBM), and Support Vector Classifier (SVC)—to predict myocardial infarction (MI) status using ten variables from the UK Biobank dataset ($N = 1500$, with 20% held out for testing). The models were developed using Python 3.11.4, Scikit-learn 1.3.0, and SHAP's official library.

The relative importance of features, as shown in Fig. 4.5, revealed consistency in the top three features across models. However, the remaining rankings diverged notably; for example, Body Mass Index ranked lowest in DT and LR but was among the top three in LGBM. Furthermore, in the DT model, the five least influential features had SHAP values near zero, indicating no effect on prediction. Interestingly, despite differences in interpretability outcomes, classification accuracy remained comparable across all models. This underscores the importance of interpreting SHAP results within the context of the specific model architecture used.

4.5.2 Grad-CAM: Explainability for Image- and Video-Based Models

While many explainability methods focus on tabular or text-based models, computer vision systems require specialized approaches to reveal how they make decisions. Gradient-weighted Class Activation Mapping (Grad-CAM) is a widely adopted method for improving

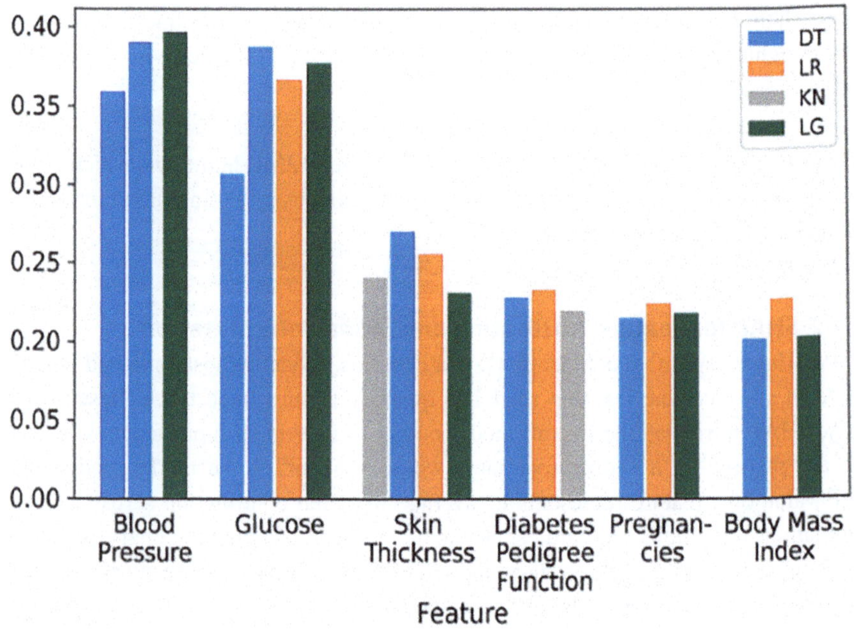

Fig. 4.5 Feature importance ranking across models

interpretability in convolutional neural networks (CNNs), particularly in models that process images and videos. Its relevance stems from the increasing demand for explainable AI in high-stakes domains such as medical imaging, recruitment, and financial decision-making, where understanding *why* a model made a prediction is as critical as the prediction itself [33]. Grad-CAM addresses this need by providing **visual explanations** that identify the regions in the input that most strongly influence a model's output, thereby bridging the gap between black-box deep learning systems and human interpretability.

Grad-CAM operates by leveraging the gradients of the target class score y^c with respect to the feature maps A^k in the final convolutional layer of a CNN. These gradients capture how sensitive the class score is to changes in each spatial location of the feature maps. The importance of each feature map is computed by applying **global average pooling** over the gradients:

$$\alpha_k^c = \frac{1}{Z}\sum_i \sum_j \frac{\partial y^c}{\partial A_{ij}^k}$$

where α_k^c is the weight assigned to the kth feature map and Z is the number of spatial locations in that map. The Grad-CAM heatmap is then produced by a weighted combination of these maps followed by a ReLU activation:

$$L^c_{\text{Grad-CAM}} = \text{ReLU}\left(\sum_k \alpha^c_k A^k\right).$$

The ReLU function ensures that only features positively contributing to the target class are highlighted. The result is a **coarse localization map** showing which regions in the input most influenced the model's prediction.

Practical Applications of Grad-CAM

- **Medical Imaging:** In pregnancy risk assessment models, Grad-CAM highlights anatomical regions of interest in ultrasound scans, enabling clinicians to verify that the model's focus aligns with medical knowledge.
- **Recruitment:** For AI-driven resume screening or facial analysis tools, Grad-CAM can reveal whether models are using relevant features, supporting fairness audits by exposing reliance on potentially discriminatory visual patterns.
- **Financial Decision-Making:** In credit scoring, Grad-CAM can be applied to visual dashboards or document analysis systems, ensuring that model decisions are traceable to appropriate features.

Benefits and Limitations Grad-CAM improves transparency by generating interpretable visualizations that support debugging, auditing, and regulatory compliance. However, it provides **coarse explanations** rather than pixel-level precision and may exhibit sensitivity to minor input perturbations, raising questions about the stability of its interpretations [34]. Thus, while Grad-CAM is a significant step toward interpretability, it is best used in conjunction with other explanation techniques such as LIME or SHAP for a comprehensive understanding.

Figure 4.6 illustrates the Grad-CAM process, a widely used technique for enhancing interpretability in convolutional neural networks applied to images and videos. As shown, the method begins by propagating gradients from the target class back to the final convolutional layers, where the resulting feature maps are weighted according to their relevance. These weighted maps are then combined to produce a heatmap, which highlights the regions of the input image most influential in the model's prediction. By overlaying this heatmap on the original input, Grad-CAM provides a visual explanation of the model's decision-making process, enabling practitioners to validate, debug, and audit AI systems used in high-stakes domains such as healthcare, recruitment, and credit scoring.

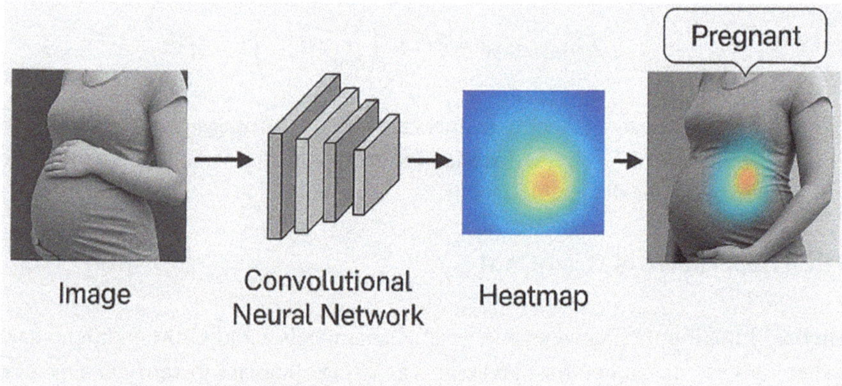

Fig. 4.6 Grad-CAM for visual explanation in pregnancy

4.6 Fairness in AI: Theoretical Foundations and Practical Implementation

4.6.1 Theoretical Foundations of Fairness

Fairness—also referred to as algorithmic justice—denotes the principle that AI systems should operate without producing systematically discriminatory outcomes, particularly against individuals or groups defined by protected attributes such as gender, race, age, or socioeconomic status. The theoretical basis of fairness draws from legal theory, moral philosophy, and social justice literature. Notably, Rawls' theory of distributive justice [35] and the formalization of individual fairness by Dwork et al. [36] provide foundational contributions.

Several conceptual models guide the operationalization of fairness:

- **Group Fairness:** Ensures parity across predefined demographic groups. Common formulations include
  - *Demographic Parity*: Equal selection or acceptance rates across groups.
  - *Equalized Odds*: Equal true positive and false positive rates for each group [37].
  - *Disparate Impact*: Avoidance of disproportionate negative outcomes for any protected group.
- **Individual Fairness:** Requires that similar individuals receive similar outcomes, assuming a domain-specific similarity metric [36].
- **Counterfactual Fairness:** A decision is considered fair if it remains unchanged in a counterfactual scenario where an individual's sensitive attributes were different [5].

To illustrate in healthcare context, group fairness is critical, particularly demographic parity and disparate impact. The model must ensure that access to care is not biased by race, income level, or region. For instance, an algorithm that disproportionately denies care to rural or low-income patients would fail the fairness test. Fair preprocessing, group parity audits, and demographic impact reports are key tools. While counterfactual fairness can be applied to test if changing a person's socioeconomic status would affect their eligibility unjustly.

In the case pregnancy risk prediction aligns with individual fairness—expectant mothers with similar health profiles should receive comparable risk scores, regardless of their age, marital status, or ethnicity. Group Fairness via equalized odds is also relevant, ensuring that the model doesn't overestimate risk for specific demographic groups, which could lead to paternalistic medical decisions. Counterfactual Fairness helps verify that sensitive attributes (e.g., being an adolescent or from an indigenous background) do not unduly alter outcomes.

In the case personal selection is a classic testbed for group Fairness, particularly demographic parity and equalized odds, to ensure selection rates are not biased by gender, age, or ethnicity. Individual fairness is crucial: candidates with similar qualifications should be treated similarly, avoiding proxy variables like zip code or university attended if they embed historical discrimination. Counterfactual fairness helps answer: would this candidate still be accepted if their gender or ethnic background were different?

In the case credit allocation equityFair lending must balance group fairness (e.g., Disparate Impact) and counterfactual fairness. Denial rates must not disproportionately affect women, minorities, or rural populations. Individual fairness ensures that applicants with similar creditworthiness receive similar evaluations, independent of non-financial characteristics. Counterfactual fairness tests and SHAP-based justifications ensure the model doesn't encode hidden discrimination.

4.6.2 Practical Implementation and Formalization

Achieving fairness in practice involves interventions at multiple stages of the machine learning lifecycle. Key techniques include

- **Bias Auditing:** Statistical assessment of training and test datasets to detect representational imbalances. Tools such as IBM AI Fairness 360, Microsoft's Fairlearn, and Google's What-If Tool support this process.
- **Fairness-Constrained Training:** Incorporating fairness constraints directly into the objective function. For instance, penalties are introduced for violating demographic parity or equalized odds during model optimization [38]. Modern approaches to fairness often employ constrained optimization, where model performance objectives are balanced against explicit fairness constraints. For example, an algorithm may minimize overall classification error while ensuring that error rates remain similar across protected

groups—a principle underlying metrics like Equalized Odds. Tools such as Microsoft's Fairlearn implement these techniques, enabling practitioners to incorporate ethical constraints directly into the model training process.

- **Post Hoc Adjustments:** Applying recalibration or threshold adjustment techniques to align output distributions with fairness metrics, without retraining the underlying model.
- **Formal Fairness Verification:** Utilizing formal methods—such as Satisfiability Modulo Theories (SMT) solvers—to verify compliance with fairness properties. Explainability tools and audit logs are also employed to support accountability.

To promote fairness and robustness in machine learning models, it is essential to apply data balancing and resampling techniques that ensure equitable representation across demographic groups. This foundational step mitigates biases stemming from imbalanced datasets and helps models learn patterns that are not skewed toward majority populations. Complementing this, fairness-aware evaluation metrics—such as Equal Opportunity, Demographic Parity, and Disparate Impact—should be systematically employed to assess whether model performance is consistent and just across all subgroups. Moreover, techniques like adversarial training and multitask learning can be leveraged to encourage the learning of invariant representations, helping the model focus on task-relevant information while ignoring spurious correlations tied to sensitive attributes. In addition, generative models (e.g., GANs or VAEs) can be used to augment underrepresented classes and reveal hidden decision boundaries, thereby enhancing generalization in low-data regimes. Finally, practitioners must be cautious to avoid common fallacies, such as mistaking correlation for causation or presuming that high overall accuracy implies fairness—especially when performance disparities persist across protected groups.

4.6.3 Operationalizing Fairness and Explainability: From Principles to Practice

One of the central objectives of this chapter is to bridge ethical principles such as fairness, transparency, and accountability with their practical implementation in real-world AI workflows. To achieve this, the accompanying scenarios—covering pregnancy risk assessment, healthcare diagnostics, recruitment systems, and credit scoring—serve as hands-on environments for applying fairness-aware modeling and explainability techniques. These scenarios move beyond abstract discussion, demonstrating how ethical concepts can be embedded into model pipelines using widely adopted frameworks such as Fairlearn, IBM AIF360, LIME, SHAP, and Grad-CAM.

4.6.3.1 Pregnancy Risk Assessment (Image-Based Models)

Explainability: Implement Grad-CAM on convolutional neural networks (CNNs) trained for pregnancy risk classification. Generate heatmaps to visualize the regions of ultrasound images most influential in the model's decision-making. This ensures alignment between model focus and medically relevant anatomical structures.
Fairness: Conduct subgroup performance analysis to ensure consistent model behavior across demographic groups (e.g., age ranges). If disparities are detected, use reweighing techniques to balance the training dataset.

4.6.3.2 Healthcare Applications (Tabular/Text Models)

Explainability: Apply LIME to provide local explanations for individual predictions (e.g., high-risk patient classifications). Complement this with SHAP for global interpretability, identifying which clinical variables most influence overall model performance.
Fairness: Use preprocessing techniques such as reweighing or optimized preprocessing when datasets are imbalanced across demographic groups. If training is accessible, integrate fairness-constrained optimization to equalize error rates across patient subgroups.

4.6.3.3 Recruitment Systems

Explainability: Use LIME to interpret individual candidate rankings, identifying key features driving classification decisions. Apply SHAP for global analysis, highlighting the influence of demographic or experience-related features on model outputs.
Fairness: Apply post-processing methods such as Equalized Odds Postprocessing to adjust outputs and reduce discrimination against protected attributes (e.g., gender or ethnicity). Where possible, incorporate adversarial debiasing into model training.

4.6.3.4 Credit Scoring Models

Explainability: Use SHAP to break down individual credit approval decisions, showing the contributions of variables like payment history, debt-to-income ratio, and employment stability. Generate global summaries to audit overall feature importance.
Fairness: Implement fairness-constrained optimization during training to enforce metrics such as Demographic Parity or Equalized Odds. For post-processing, use Reject Option Classification to adjust borderline decisions, ensuring equitable outcomes for disadvantaged groups.

Table 4.2 summarizes the application of fairness and explainability techniques across the Colab exercises, linking each method to its domain-specific use case and the ethical principles it operationalizes. This synthesis highlights how abstract ethical values can be translated into concrete, auditable AI workflows.

These implementations transform ethical principles into actionable workflows, enabling practitioners to evaluate, debug, and audit models in high-stakes domains. By integrating

Table 4.2 Operationalizing fairness and explainability techniques across USAID ethical scenarios

Technique	Domain	Application	Ethical principle operationalized
Grad-CAM	Pregnancy risk assessment	Visualizing model attention in ultrasound-based classification	Transparency, accountability
LIME/SHAP	Healthcare	Explaining patient risk predictions and identifying key variables	Transparency, explainability
LIME/SHAP	Recruitment	Interpreting candidate ranking decisions	Fairness, transparency
SHAP	Credit Scoring	Explaining individual credit decisions and global model behavior	Accountability, Fairness
Fairness-constrained optimization	Healthcare/Credit scoring	Ensuring parity in error rates across subgroups	Fairness, non-discrimination
Postprocessing (Equalized odds/Reject option)	Recruitment/Credit	Adjusting outputs to reduce discrimination	Fairness, justice

fairness and explainability into each stage of the model lifecycle, the exercises provide a concrete roadmap for building AI systems that are both technically robust and ethically grounded.

Explaining the SHAP Code

SHAP (SHapley Additive exPlanations), a widely used library for interpreting Machine Learning models. It helps understand the contribution of each feature to individual model predictions.

SHAP Code

```
explainer = shap.TreeExplainer(model)
shap_values = explainer.shap_values(X_test)
print("Shap_values:", type(shap_values))
```

Line-by-Line Explanation

1. `explainer = shap.TreeExplainer(model)`
   This creates a **SHAP explainer** for a pre-trained model (`model`). The `TreeExplainer` is specifically optimized for *tree-based models* such as Random Forest, XGBoost, or LightGBM. Its purpose is to calculate the **contribution of each feature** to the model's predictions.
2. `shap_values = explainer.shap_values(X_test)`
   This computes the **SHAP values** for the dataset `X_test`. Each SHAP value indicates the **individual impact of a feature** on the prediction for a particular observation. This helps answer the question: *"Why did the model make this prediction for this instance?"*
3. `print("Shap_values:", type(shap_values))`
   This prints the **type of the SHAP values** (often a `numpy.ndarray` or a list of arrays, depending on the model). This step helps verify the structure before visualization or further processing.

Importance of SHAP Values

- **Model Interpretability:** SHAP provides insights into which features are driving predictions.
- **Ethics and Auditing:** Useful for ensuring that models make transparent and unbiased decisions, especially in sensitive domains such as finance, healthcare, and hiring.
- **Visualization:** SHAP values can be plotted using built-in functions (e.g., `shap.summary_plot`, `shap.force_plot`) to visually interpret feature importance and effects.

Explaining the Fairlearn Code

Fairlearn is a Python library used to *detect and mitigate bias* in machine learning models. It provides tools for evaluating model fairness and implementing algorithms that adjust model behavior to meet ethical or regulatory requirements.

- **ExponentiatedGradient:** A fairness-aware reduction algorithm that adjusts a model to satisfy specified fairness constraints. It iteratively reweights training data to reduce disparities across protected groups.
- **DemographicParity:** A fairness constraint that ensures similar outcomes across groups (e.g., gender or race). It is particularly useful for *bias mitigation* in classification tasks, where fairness across sensitive attributes is critical.

Fairlearn

```
import pandas as pd
from fairlearn.reductions import ExponentiatedGradient, DemographicParity
from sklearn.metrics import confusion_matrix
```

4.7 Key Takeaways

- **Ethical principles in AI**—such as fairness, transparency, and accountability—can be rigorously translated into mathematical constraints and verifiable properties, making them enforceable within model design and evaluation.
- **Formal verification tools** (e.g., TLA+, Alloy, model checkers) and fairness toolkits (e.g., Fairlearn, AIF360) provide practical frameworks to **audit, test, and enforce these ethical principles** in real-world AI systems.
- **Operationalizing ethics** through explainability techniques (LIME, SHAP, Grad-CAM) and fairness-aware optimization bridges the gap between abstract values and applied engineering practice.
- **Security and resilience are essential ethical imperatives**: Chapter 4 also emphasizes threat modeling, adversarial robustness, and resilience mechanisms, ensuring that AI systems remain trustworthy in adversarial environments.

Chapter 5 will focus on the role of security as a verifiable ethical imperative in AI, including threat modeling and resilience against adversarial attacks.

References

1. Angwin, J., Larson, J., Mattu, S., & Kirchner, L. (2016). Machine bias: There's software used across the country to predict future criminals. And it's biased against Blacks. *ProPublica*. https://www.propublica.org/article/machine-bias-risk-assessments-in-criminal-sentencing
2. Mehrabi, N., Morstatter, F., Saxena, N., Lerman, K., & Galstyan, A. (2020). Fairness and machine learning: Limitations and opportunities [PDF].
3. Bolukbasi, T., Chang, K.-W., Zou, J., Saligrama, V., & Kalai, A. (2016). Man is to computer programmer as woman is to homemaker? Debiasing word embeddings. *Proceedings of the 30th International Conference on Neural Information Processing Systems (NIPS'16)*, 4356–4364.
4. Bartlett, R., Morse, A., Stanton, R. H., & Wallace, N. E. (2019). Consumer-lending discrimination in the FinTech era (NBER Working Paper No. w25943). National Bureau of Economic Research; Social Science Research Network. https://papers.ssrn.com/sol3/papers.cfm?abstract_id=3491267
5. Kusner, M. J., Loftus, J., Russell, C., & Silva, R. (2017). Counterfactual fairness. In *Advances in Neural Information Processing Systems* (pp. 4066–4076).

6. Covington, P., Covington, P., Adams, J., & Sargin, E. (2016). Deep neural networks for YouTube recommendations. YouTube Tech Blog / Proceedings of the ACM Conference on Recommender Systems (RecSys '16). https://www.researchgate.net/publication/307573656_Deep_Neural_Networks_for_YouTube_Recommendations
7. Gao, Y., Liu, F., & Gao, L. (2023). Echo chamber effects on short video platforms. Scientific Reports, 13, Article 6282. https://doi.org/10.1038/s41598-023-33370-1
8. Roy, I., & Sengupta, M. (2023). Digital echo chambers: The amplification of identity politics in social media platforms. *Proceedings*, 546–554.
9. Jain, L. R., & Menon, V. (2023). AI algorithmic bias: Understanding its causes, ethical and social implications. En Proceedings of the 35th IEEE International Conference on Tools with Artificial Intelligence (ICTAI 2023) (pp. 460–467). IEEE. https://doi.org/10.1109/ICTAI59109.2023.00073
10. Dominguez-Catena, I., Paternain, D., & Galar, M. (2024). Metrics for dataset demographic bias: A case study on facial expression recognition. IEEE Transactions on Pattern Analysis and Machine Intelligence, 46(8), 5209–5226. https://doi.org/10.1109/TPAMI.2024.3361979
11. Mansilla, L., Claucich, E., Echeveste, R., & Ferrante, E. (2024). Demographically-Informed Prediction Discrepancy Index: Early Warnings of Demographic Biases for Unlabeled Populations. *Transactions on Machine Learning Research.*
12. Leino, K., Black, E., Fredrikson, M., Sen, S., & Datta, A. (2019). Feature-wise bias amplification (arXiv:1812.08999). arXiv. https://doi.org/10.48550/arXiv.1812.08999
13. Wang, A., & Russakovsky, O. (2021). Directional bias amplification (arXiv:2102.12594). arXiv. https://doi.org/10.48550/arXiv.2102.12594
14. Abusitta, A., Aïmeur, E., & Abdel Wahab, O. (2019). Generative adversarial networks for mitigating biases in machine learning systems (arXiv:1905.09972). arXiv. https://doi.org/10.48550/arXiv.1905.09972
15. Groh, M., Harris, C., Soenksen, L., Badri, O., et al. (2021). Evaluating deep neural networks trained on clinical images in dermatology with the Fitzpatrick 17k dataset. In *IEEE CVPR Workshops.*
16. Muthua, A. G., Theart, R. P., & Booysen, M. J. (2023). Using infrared to improve face recognition of individuals with highly pigmented skin. iScience, 26(7), Article 107039. https://doi.org/10.1016/j.isci.2023.107039
17. Farooq, S., Abbas, S., Abid, A., & Rasheed, S. (2021). A hybrid algorithm for face detection to avoid racial inequity due to dark skin. IEEE Access, 9, 150734–150746. https://doi.org/10.1109/ACCESS.2021.3122870
18. Zhang, W., Zhou, S., Walsh, T., & Weiss, J. C. (2025). Fairness amidst non-IID graph data: A literature review (arXiv:2202.07170). arXiv. https://doi.org/10.48550/arXiv.2202.07170
19. Irfan, Z., McCaffery, F., & Loughran, R. (2023). Evaluating fairness metrics. En L. Boratto, et al. (Eds.), Advances in Bias and Fairness in Information Retrieval (Communications in Computer and Information Science, Vol. 1840, pp. 31–41). Springer. https://doi.org/10.1007/978-3-031-37249-0_3
20. Na, A. (2025). Identification Improvement of Malignant Skin Diseases for Diverse Skin Tones with Grad-CAM. In: Palaiahnakote, S., Schuckers, S., Ogier, JM., Bhattacharya, P., Pal, U., Bhattacharya, S. (eds) Pattern Recognition. ICPR 2024 International Workshops and Challenges. ICPR 2024. Lecture Notes in Computer Science, vol 15615. Springer, Cham. https://doi.org/10.1007/978-3-031-87660-8_10
21. Krishnan, A., Neas, B., & Rattani, A. (2022). Is facial recognition biased at near-infrared spectrum as well? (arXiv:2211.00129). arXiv. https://doi.org/10.48550/arXiv.2211.00129
22. Haliburton, L., Leusmann, J., Welsch, R. et al. Uncovering labeler bias in machine learning annotation tasks. AI Ethics 5, 2515–2528 (2025). https://doi.org/10.1007/s43681-024-00572-w

23. Zhioua, S., & Binkytė, R. (2023). Shedding light on underrepresentation and sampling bias in machine learning (arXiv:2306.05068). arXiv. https://doi.org/10.48550/arXiv.2306.05068
24. Hassan, Eman. (2006). Recall Bias can be a Threat to Retrospective and Prospective Research Designs. Internet Journal of Epidemiology. 3. 4. 10.5580/2732.
25. Favier, M., Calders, T., Pinxteren, S. et al. How to be fair? A study of label and selection bias. Mach Learn 112, 5081–5104 (2023). https://doi.org/10.1007/s10994-023-06401-1
26. Mourali, M., Novakowski, D., Pogacar, R., & Brigden, N. (2025). Public perception of accuracy-fairness trade-offs in algorithmic decisions in the United States. *PLoS ONE.*
27. Fu, Runshan and Aseri, Manmohan and Singh, Param Vir and Srinivasan, Kannan, 'Un'Fair Machine Learning Algorithms (June 10, 2020). Available at SSRN: https://ssrn.com/abstract=3408275 or https://doi.org/10.2139/ssrn.3408275
28. Skliarov, M., Shawi, R.E., Dhaoui, C. et al. A comparative evaluation of explainability techniques for image data. Sci Rep 15, 41898 (2025). https://doi.org/10.1038/s41598-025-25839-y
29. F. R. Falvo and M. Cannataro, "Explainability techniques for Artificial Intelligence models in medical diagnostic," in 2024 IEEE International Conference on Bioinformatics and Biomedicine (BIBM), Lisbon, Portugal, 2024, pp. 6907-6913, https://doi.org/10.1109/BIBM62325.2024.10821826.
30. Salih, A. M., Raisi-Estabragh, Z., Galazzo, I. B., Radeva, P., Petersen, S. E., Lekadir, K., & Menegaz, G. (2024). A perspective on explainable artificial intelligence methods: SHAP and LIME. Advanced Intelligent Systems, 7(1), Article e2400304. https://doi.org/10.1002/aisy.202400304
31. Barbudo Carrasco, L. (2025). Mitigating Bias and Advocating for Data Sovereignty: The Role of Metadata and Paradata in Ethical AI-Driven Information Systems. *Journal of Library Metadata.*
32. Miguel, B.S., Naseer, A., & Inakoshi, H. (2020). Putting Accountability of AI Systems into Practice. In *Proceedings of the IJCAI International Joint Conference on Artificial Intelligence.*
33. Selvaraju, R. R., Cogswell, M., Das, A., Vedantam, R., Parikh, D., & Batra, D. (2017). Grad-CAM: Visual Explanations from Deep Networks via Gradient-based Localization. In *Proceedings of the IEEE International Conference on Computer Vision (ICCV).*
34. Adebayo, Adebayo, J., Gilmer, J., Muelly, M., Goodfellow, I., Hardt, M., & Kim, B. (2020). Sanity checks for saliency maps (arXiv:1810.03292). arXiv. https://doi.org/10.48550/arXiv.1810.03292.
35. Frohlich, N., Oppenheimer, J. A., & Eavey, C. L. (1987). Laboratory results on Rawls's distributive justice. The Journal of Politics, 49(4), 1187–1208. Retrieved from https://www.jstor.org/stable/193962
36. Dwork, C., Hardt, M., Pitassi, T., Reingold, O., & Zemel, R. (2012). Fairness through awareness. En Proceedings of the 3rd Innovations in Theoretical Computer Science Conference (ITCS 2012) (pp. 214–226). Association for Computing Machinery. https://doi.org/10.1145/2090236.2090255
37. Hardt, M., Price, E., & Srebro, N. (2016). Equality of opportunity in supervised learning. In *Advances in Neural Information Processing Systems* (pp. 3315–3323).
38. Zafar, M. B., Valera, I., Gomez Rodriguez, M., & Gummadi, K. P. (2017). Fairness constraints: Mechanisms for fair classification. In *Artificial Intelligence and Statistics* (pp. 962–970).
39. Zhenpeng Chen, Jie M. Zhang, Max Hort, Mark Harman, and Federica Sarro. 2024. Fairness Testing: A Comprehensive Survey and Analysis of Trends. ACM Trans. Softw. Eng. Methodol. 33, 5, Article 137 (June 2024), 59 pages. https://doi.org/10.1145/3652155

Part II
Governing AI in the Wild: Security, Law, and Resilience

As AI systems exit controlled lab environments and enter complex, unpredictable real-world settings, governance becomes both an ethical mandate and a practical necessity. Part II focuses on the mechanisms and frameworks required to safeguard AI deployment at scale—where failures can amplify inequality, compromise national security, or erode public trust. The chapters in this section delve into cybersecurity threats specific to machine learning models, the dual-use risks of generative AI, and the evolution of legal instruments such as the EU AI Act. Furthermore, this part presents strategies for multilevel governance, systemic resilience, and risk-aware regulation. It underscores the importance of moving beyond compliance checklists toward proactive, context-aware governance models that are transparent, adaptive, and globally interoperable.

Security as an Ethical Imperative in AI Systems 5

5.1 Security as an Ethical Imperative in AI Systems

The phenomenon of GPT-3 jailbreaking between 2022 and 2023 exposed critical vulnerabilities in the safety mechanisms of large language models (LLMs), underscoring the urgent need for robust governance and technical safeguards. Researchers demonstrated that with carefully crafted prompts or adversarial inputs, it was possible to bypass embedded safety guardrails, thereby coercing models like GPT-3 into generating outputs that violated ethical and legal norms—including hate speech, misinformation, and step-by-step instructions for criminal acts [1, 2]. This not only challenges assumptions about the reliability of content moderation via fine-tuning and reinforcement learning with human feedback (RLHF), but also raises profound ethical questions regarding responsibility and liability in generative AI deployment [3]. The ease with which these models can be manipulated suggests that post-deployment oversight and adversarial red-teaming must be institutionalized within AI lifecycle management, and that existing alignment strategies remain insufficient in the face of emergent jailbreaking techniques [4]. As a result, the discourse around AI safety is increasingly converging with cybersecurity paradigms, emphasizing the need for defense-in-depth architectures and explainable mitigation strategies for LLM vulnerabilities [5].

While safety in artificial intelligence (AI) systems traditionally refers to the prevention of unintentional failures—such as system crashes, misclassifications due to noise, or poor generalization to unseen data—security encompasses a broader class of concerns rooted in intentional, adversarial behavior that seeks to subvert the intended objectives of the system. This distinction is critical because safety failures are often a result of system complexity or environmental uncertainty, whereas security breaches result from strategic manipulation by an intelligent adversary who actively exploits vulnerabilities in the system's design, learning process, or deployment context.

R. Andrade et al., *Building Ethical and Secure AI*, Synthesis Lectures on Computer Science,
https://doi.org/10.1007/978-3-032-25789-5_5

Table 5.1 Comparison of safety and security concerns in AI systems

Safety concerns	Security concerns
Unintentional system failures	Intentional adversarial manipulation
Algorithm misclassifications	Strategic exploitation of vulnerabilities
Poor generalization to new data	Attacks on training data or model architecture
Emergent behaviors from complex systems	Deliberate subversion of system objectives

As illustrated in Table 5.1, safety concerns typically arise from unintended consequences, such as system failures, algorithmic misclassifications, or poor generalization, which often stem from limitations in training data or model complexity. In contrast, security concerns reflect intentional adversarial behaviors, including data poisoning, manipulation of model architectures, or the deliberate subversion of system goals.

To ensure the trustworthy deployment of AI systems, it is essential to prioritize three core imperatives that underpin safety, reliability, and ethical compliance

1. **Protection of vulnerable populations** is essential, as AI security failures disproportionately affect marginalized communities that often lack adequate resources to seek redress or recover from harm.
2. **Preservation of trust** is vital in sustaining public confidence in AI technologies; widespread breaches or systemic vulnerabilities may erode this trust and hinder the adoption of potentially beneficial innovations.
3. **Prevention of dual-use exploitation** safeguards society from the malicious repurposing of AI, where tools designed for beneficial applications could be transformed into instruments for surveillance, manipulation, or discrimination.

Artificial intelligence systems, especially those grounded in machine learning paradigms, diverge significantly from traditional software in their architecture, operational logic, and deployment models. Unlike conventional rule-based systems, machine learning models acquire behavior through exposure to data, making them inherently susceptible to manipulation via the training or inference phases. This data dependency introduces unprecedented security risks, including but not limited to data poisoning (where malicious inputs compromise the model during training), adversarial examples (inputs subtly altered to deceive AI systems), and model extraction or theft (unauthorized replication of proprietary models through exposed APIs or outputs) [6–8].

These vulnerabilities cannot be mitigated through classical security paradigms alone; rather, they require a reconceptualization of AI security as a multidisciplinary endeavor. In response, the introduction calls for policymakers, engineers, and academic researchers to establish new frameworks of technical hardening, continuous model verification, and legal accountability. This shift is essential to ensure that AI development proceeds with

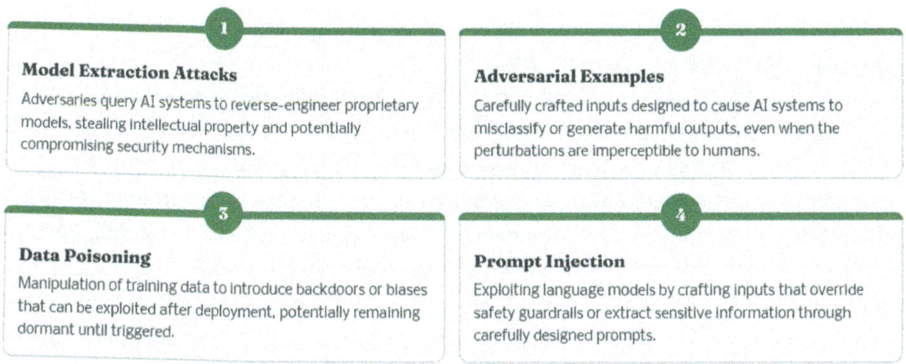

Fig. 5.1 Evolving threat landscape

resilience, transparency, and safety at its core, particularly as these systems begin to operate in high-stakes domains such as defense, healthcare, and critical infrastructure.

Figure 5.1 outlines four major security threats targeting AI systems, each representing a distinct form of vulnerability exploitation. Model-extraction attacks involve reverse-engineering proprietary models to compromise intellectual property and internal defense mechanisms. Adversarial examples deceive models through imperceptible perturbations, forcing misclassifications or unsafe behavior. Data poisoning undermines model integrity by manipulating training data to introduce hidden backdoors or systemic biases. Finally, prompt injection specifically threatens large language models by bypassing predefined safety constraints or eliciting confidential information. These categories exemplify the evolving threat landscape AI systems must withstand and emphasize the need for integrated security-by-design methodologies in the development pipeline [6].

In AI systems, adversarial threats manifest in diverse ways, each challenging core principles of trustworthy computing:

- Adversarial Examples exploit the non-linear decision boundaries of machine learning models. By introducing imperceptibly small but precisely crafted perturbations to input data, attackers can induce targeted misclassifications while preserving visual or semantic similarity to benign samples [9]. This undermines model integrity, as the system produces erroneous outputs even under seemingly valid inputs. The fragility is particularly acute in high-dimensional spaces like vision and language, where decision boundaries are complex and difficult to characterize formally.
- Model Extraction Attacks attempt to replicate the behavior of a proprietary model by issuing structured queries to its API and observing the responses [10]. Over time, attackers can approximate the decision function, enabling downstream misuse such as re-identification, unauthorized redistribution, or white-box adversarial generation. This

threatens the confidentiality and intellectual property of AI models, particularly in cloud-deployed inference-as-a-service settings.

- Data Poisoning Attacks intervene during the model training phase by inserting carefully crafted data instances into the training set with the goal of corrupting the learned model parameters or introducing targeted backdoors [8]. These attacks compromise availability and reliability, enabling malicious agents to degrade model performance or trigger harmful behavior on demand. In federated learning or crowdsourced training contexts, poisoning risks are amplified due to lack of centralized data vetting.
- Prompt Injection refers to a type of adversarial attack against language models (e.g., GPT-based systems), where malicious actors craft inputs that manipulate the model's behavior by injecting unauthorized instructions or overriding intended constraints [11]. These attacks exploit the model's inability to distinguish between genuine user prompts and hidden directives embedded in the input, potentially causing the model to produce harmful, unintended, or unauthorized outputs.

These threat vectors expose a structural vulnerability in current AI design pipelines, which often assume benign data distributions and overlook strategic manipulation. From a cybersecurity perspective, adversarial machine learning necessitates a paradigm shift: integrating robust learning theory, formal verification, and threat modeling into ML system design. At the same time, these vulnerabilities have direct implications for human rights and ethical engineering, particularly when AI systems are deployed in high-stakes contexts such as medical diagnosis, criminal justice, or social welfare. Attacks that compromise fairness, privacy, or accountability ultimately erode the legitimacy of AI systems in democratic societies.

Therefore, aligning AI security with human-rights-aligned engineering involves not only hardening technical components but also anticipating misuse scenarios, establishing auditability and redress mechanisms, and embedding security-by-design principles into AI governance frameworks [3]. As AI becomes increasingly integrated into critical infrastructures, the dual imperative of robustness and rights-respectful design becomes foundational to both system dependability and public trust.

5.2 Cybersecurity Attacks in Artificial Intelligence

5.2.1 Model Extraction Attacks and Intellectual Property Risks

Model-extraction (or "model-stealing") attacks occur when an adversary—armed only with query access to a deployed machine learning model—systematically infers a high-fidelity surrogate that approximates the victim model's decision function. In the canonical threat model proposed by Tramér et al. [10], the attacker iteratively issues strategically crafted inputs, collects the corresponding outputs (class labels, confidence scores, or logits), and uses the input-output pairs to train a replica. Subsequent research has refined this paradigm along two axes:

- **Query Efficiency**: Adaptive strategies such as Jacobian-based dataset augmentation [12] and active learning based on uncertainty sampling [13] reduce the number of required queries, achieving high-fidelity extraction with minimal API calls.
- **Output Granularity**: Access to full probability vectors drastically simplifies replication, whereas label-only interfaces require sophisticated query synthesis [14].

The consequences extend beyond intellectual property theft. Attackers with surrogate models can:

- Generate *white-box adversarial examples* transferable to the original.
- Perform *membership-inference attacks*, compromising training-data privacy.
- Embed the stolen model in rival products, bypassing licensing or attribution [15].

These attacks jeopardize the confidentiality and integrity of models, particularly in inference-as-a-service contexts. From a human rights standpoint, extracted models may be repurposed for surveillance, profiling, or other harmful applications.

To mitigate these risks, technical and organizational controls are necessary:

- **API Hardening**: Restrict access to confidence scores or introduce output noise.
- **Watermarking**: Embed invisible model signatures to support IP protection.
- **Query Monitoring**: Detect abnormal query patterns using statistical detectors.
- **Secure Execution**: Use TEEs or encrypted inference to prevent memory exposure.

From a regulatory perspective, model-extraction threats are acknowledged in emerging AI governance.

5.2.2 Data Poisoning Attacks and the Corruption of the Learning Process

Data poisoning attacks exploit the vulnerability of machine learning algorithms to compromised training data. By injecting maliciously crafted samples into the training dataset, adversaries can alter the decision boundaries of the model, degrade its accuracy, or embed backdoors that trigger harmful behavior under specific conditions [8, 16]. Unlike evasion attacks that occur at inference time, poisoning operates upstream, corrupting the training process itself.

These attacks typically fall into two main categories:

- **Availability Attacks**: Aim to degrade overall model performance by introducing label noise or outlier features that destabilize convergence [17].
- **Integrity Attacks (Backdoors)**: Insert inputs with hidden triggers such that, during inference, the presence of the trigger induces a specific misclassification while preserving normal performance on clean data [18].

The threat is particularly acute in modern training paradigms such as:

- **Federated Learning**: Multiple clients train locally and aggregate updates, which opens the door to model poisoning via manipulated gradients without centralized inspection [19].
- **Data Marketplaces and Web-Crawled Corpora**: Open or weakly curated sources increase exposure to malicious injection, especially in large-scale foundation models [20].

The ethical and security implications are profound. Data poisoning undermines reliability, erodes user trust, and creates covert channels for manipulation. In critical domains such as autonomous driving or healthcare, a backdoored model can cause catastrophic failures while eluding conventional validation metrics.

Mitigation strategies span technical and organizational layers:

- **Robust Training**: Use of noise-tolerant loss functions, data sanitization, or influence functions to detect anomalous samples.
- **Differential Privacy**: Introduces statistical noise that can obscure individual sample influence, limiting the effect of poison points.
- **Certified Defenses**: Formal methods to bound model deviation under bounded poisoning rates.

From a governance standpoint, ISO/IEC 23894 and the EU AI Act emphasize the need for traceability.

5.3 OWASP Top 10 Security Risks for Large Language Model Applications

5.3.1 Prompt Injection

Prompt Injection is a critical vulnerability wherein an attacker crafts input prompts to manipulate the behavior of the language model, often bypassing intended system instructions. By embedding malicious directives or natural language that the model interprets as part of its functional logic, attackers can elicit unauthorized actions or access restricted data. This risk is heightened in applications where user input is concatenated with system prompts without proper input sanitization or separation.

5.3.2 Insecure Output Handling

Insecure output handling arises when LLM-generated responses are rendered or executed without adequate validation. Outputs may include URLs, code snippets, shell commands, or HTML that, if blindly trusted, could trigger client-side attacks such as Cross-Site Scripting (XSS), server-side request forgery (SSRF), or even command injection. This risk mandates strong output validation and contextual awareness before rendering or executing LLM responses.

5.3.3 Training Data Poisoning

Training Data Poisoning involves the deliberate insertion of malicious or biased data into the model's training corpus. This manipulates the behavior of the LLM post-deployment, potentially inserting backdoors or bias into outputs. It is especially dangerous in community-driven or crowdsourced datasets where data vetting is minimal. Mitigations include robust data provenance checks, differential training validation, and continuous monitoring.

5.3.4 Model Denial of Service (DoS)

LLMs are susceptible to prompt-based DoS attacks where adversaries craft inputs that exhaust system resources. These prompts may be computationally complex, recursive, or deeply nested, causing excessive CPU, GPU, or memory consumption. As a result, the system becomes unavailable to legitimate users. Defenses include input rate limiting, prompt complexity analysis, and resource bounding during inference.

5.3.5 Supply Chain Vulnerabilities

The LLM development lifecycle often involves third-party datasets, pre-trained models, and libraries. If any of these components are compromised, the entire application may inherit vulnerabilities. This includes poisoned datasets, tampered model weights, or libraries with known exploits. A secure supply chain requires provenance tracking, cryptographic verification, and regular dependency audits.

5.3.6 Sensitive Information Disclosure

LLMs trained on large-scale datasets may inadvertently memorize and output sensitive information such as API keys, personal data, or proprietary content. This risk becomes pronounced when models are exposed via public APIs. Defensive strategies involve training on sanitized datasets, implementing strict output filtering, and using differential privacy techniques.

5.3.7 Insecure Plugin Ecosystem

Modern LLM environments often integrate plugins or external tools (e.g., calculators, APIs, file systems). Without robust authentication and input/output validation, plugins become attack vectors. For example, an LLM could be tricked into making harmful API calls or executing unintended actions. A secure plugin ecosystem mandates isolation, permission scoping, and robust interface controls.

5.3.8 Excessive Agency

Excessive Agency refers to scenarios where LLMs are granted autonomous control over systems or workflows, such as sending emails or executing commands. If not constrained, this autonomy can lead to unintended operations, data exfiltration, or service disruptions. Techniques like sandboxing, human-in-the-loop control, and action gating are essential mitigations.

5.4 Integrating Security Into the AI Development Pipeline

Ensuring security throughout the entire AI lifecycle is essential for building trustworthy and resilient systems. As depicted in Fig. 5.2, a holistic security strategy must address distinct but interconnected phases, including data collection, model development, deployment, and feedback. During data collection and curation, implementing provenance tracking and integrity verification helps prevent data poisoning and ensures representativeness. In the model development phase, robustness can be enhanced through adversarial training and formal verification methods, which reduce the susceptibility to manipulated inputs and attack vectors. Secure deployment practices include continuous monitoring and defensive architectures that can detect and mitigate exploitation attempts in real time. Finally, post-deployment mechanisms such as transparent reporting channels and rapid incident response protocols enable the system to adapt dynamically to emerging threats. This lifecycle-oriented approach

Fig. 5.2 Security throughout the AI lifecycle

aligns with the broader perspective advocated in AI risk governance literature, emphasizing proactive defense and adaptability across all development stages [3, 11].

5.4.1 Overreliance

Overreliance is a socio-technical risk where users treat LLM outputs as authoritative without verification. This is particularly problematic in high-stakes domains like law, medicine, or finance, where hallucinated facts or misleading responses can have severe consequences. Responsible design should incorporate uncertainty quantification, response disclaimers, and encourage user skepticism.

5.4.2 Model Theft

Model Theft involves adversaries querying a proprietary LLM extensively to reconstruct its parameters or decision boundaries, a process also known as model extraction. This can compromise intellectual property, facilitate adversarial attacks, or enable unauthorized replication. Mitigation strategies include query rate limiting, output watermarking, and model fingerprinting to detect unauthorized use.

5.4.3 Attack Surface Modeling

The move from conventional software security to cybersecurity in artificial intelligence environments demands a new conceptual lens. Large language models (LLMs) exhibit *algorithmic complexity* whose decision boundaries are not fully auditable, rendering them vulnerable to subtle manipulations such as adversarial perturbations [9]. In parallel, *emerging attack classes*—notably data poisoning that corrupts training corpora [8] and model-extraction techniques that clone proprietary models via API queries [10]—introduce threat vectors absent from classical software stacks. Compounding these technical risks is *weak governance*: without robust traceability, version control, and provenance tracking, it is difficult to enforce foundational security properties like confidentiality and integrity across an AI pipeline. Addressing this landscape requires a *multidisciplinary security engineering approach* that blends secure architecture principles (e.g., IEEE 2413), risk-management standards tailored to AI, such as ISO/IEC 23894, and formal verification methods—ranging from SMT solving to temporal-logic model checking—to automate the proof that critical ethical and safety constraints hold in all operational states.

IEEE's proposed standard P7009 on the governance of autonomous and intelligent systems similarly highlights the importance of contextual adaptation. It emphasizes that AI policies must incorporate socio-cultural values, legal constraints, and dynamic human preferences, ensuring that system behaviors respect contextually grounded expectations. This implies not only technical configurability but also governance architectures capable of monitoring and modifying policy enforcement in response to evolving conditions[21].

To effectively mitigate the evolving landscape of AI threats, a combination of complementary technical defenses has emerged as critical for operationalizing trustworthy machine learning. Adversarial training strengthens model robustness by exposing algorithms to intentionally crafted adversarial examples during the training phase, which enhances resistance against unforeseen perturbations by up to 45%, particularly in high-risk domains such as autonomous navigation and medical diagnosis [22, 23]. In parallel, differential privacy introduces calibrated noise to training data or model outputs, offering strong theoretical guarantees against information leakage while maintaining predictive utility—a principle already adopted in production systems by leading organizations such as Apple and Google [24, 25]. Beyond training-time defenses, runtime monitoring ensures real-time anomaly detection and behavioral integrity through continuous observation of model inputs and outputs, enabling rapid detection of adversarial compromise, as demonstrated in Microsoft's AI security initiatives [3, 26]. Finally, formal verification techniques provide mathematical guarantees that AI systems adhere to safety-critical specifications and do not exceed predefined operational boundaries. Although computationally intensive, these methods have proven highly effective in applications such as aerospace and autonomous vehicles, where verification has eliminated entire classes of failure modes [27]. Collectively, these approaches represent a layered defense model aligned with the principles of explainability, accountability, and resilience in AI governance frameworks (Fig. 5.3).

In summary, context-aware policies bridge the gap between abstract ethical principles and concrete operational decisions in AI systems. They embody a socio-technical approach to AI governance, acknowledging that trustworthiness, safety, and fairness are not static properties but dynamically situated obligations.

Formalizable constraints can be layered onto each component to define invariants and trusted boundaries.

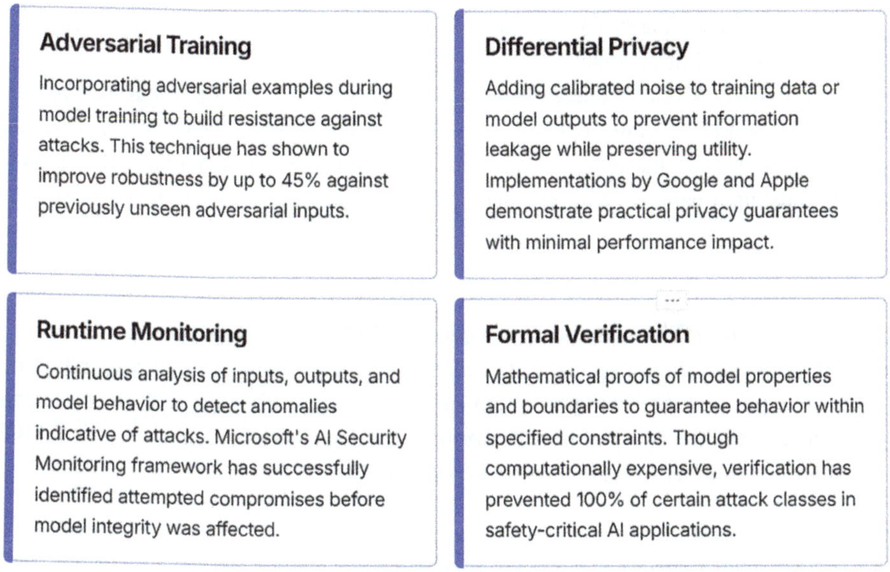

Fig. 5.3 Defensive strategies and countermeasures

5.4.4 Operationalizing Security

Building on the ethical foundations of fairness and explainability is essential to integrate security. Each of the four scenarios—pregnancy risk assessment, healthcare applications, recruitment systems, and credit scoring—operates in high-stakes domains where breaches in confidentiality, model integrity, or resilience can directly harm individuals and communities. Security in these contexts is not only a technical necessity but also a moral obligation, ensuring trust, non-maleficence, and justice in AI-driven decision-making.

5.4.4.1 Security Threats and Mitigations per Context

- **Pregnancy Risk Assessment (Image-Based Models)**: These systems are vulnerable to *data poisoning* (injection of corrupted images) and *adversarial examples* that mislead diagnosis. Mitigations include adversarial training for convolutional models, differential privacy to protect sensitive imaging data, and robust anomaly detection pipelines to flag abnormal inputs.
- **Healthcare Applications (Tabular/Text Models)**: Risks include *membership-inference attacks* that extract sensitive patient information and *model extraction* by malicious actors. Mitigations include privacy-preserving techniques (e.g., differential privacy and federated learning) and access controls with strict auditing mechanisms.
- **Recruitment Systems**: These platforms face *model inversion attacks* that reconstruct sensitive candidate profiles and *prompt injection* in interactive systems. Mitigations include

secure API management, adversarial robustness testing, and red-teaming exercises to uncover bias-exploiting attacks.

- **Credit Scoring Models**: These systems are targets for *adversarial input manipulation* (altering features to gain approval) and *data poisoning* that skews risk assessments. Mitigations include fairness-aware adversarial training, runtime anomaly detection for suspicious input patterns, and post-deployment monitoring for performance drift.

5.4.4.2 Crosswalk: Threats, Mitigations, and Ethical Imperatives

Table 5.2 maps the primary security risks identified in each context to corresponding mitigation strategies and their underlying ethical imperatives. This crosswalk illustrates how security measures directly operationalize principles such as non-maleficence, privacy, fairness, and accountability in high-stakes AI contexts [28].

5.4.4.3 From Security to Ethical Governance

Incorporating these mitigation strategies demonstrates that **security is inseparable from ethical AI governance**. By embedding differential privacy, adversarial robustness, and continuous monitoring into the development pipeline, these exercises illustrate how ethical principles—such as privacy, fairness, and non-maleficence—can be **operationalized as concrete, auditable security measures**. This alignment directly supports the emerging regulatory frameworks discussed in this chapter, including the NIST AI RMF, ISO/IEC 42001, and the EU AI Act.

Table 5.2 Operationalizing security as an ethical imperative

Context	Primary security risks	Mitigation strategies	Ethical imperative
Pregnancy risk assessment	Data poisoning; adversarial image perturbations	Adversarial training; differential privacy; anomaly detection	Non-maleficence; trust
Healthcare applications	Membership inference; model extraction	Differential privacy; federated learning; access control	Privacy; accountability
Recruitment systems	Model inversion; prompt injection	API security; adversarial robustness testing; red-teaming	Justice; fairness
Credit scoring	Adversarial manipulation; data poisoning	Fairness-aware adversarial training; runtime anomaly detection	Fairness; transparency

5.5 Key Takeaways

- **Security is an ethical imperative**: Protecting AI systems against attacks is not only a technical task but a moral obligation to uphold trust, prevent harm, and safeguard fundamental rights.
- **Threats are diverse and domain-specific**: From *data poisoning in healthcare* to *model inversion in recruitment systems*, adversaries exploit weaknesses that can directly harm individuals and communities.
- **Mitigation must be multi-layered**: Techniques such as *adversarial training, differential privacy, federated learning, and runtime anomaly detection* should be integrated throughout the AI lifecycle to ensure resilience.
- **Security aligns with ethical principles**: Each defense measure operationalizes key values such as *non-maleficence, privacy, fairness, accountability, and transparency*, transforming abstract ethics into concrete safeguards.
- **Practical application matters**: The *Colab exercises* (pregnancy risk assessment, healthcare applications, recruitment systems, and credit scoring) provide actionable contexts for embedding these security principles into real-world AI workflows.

References

1. Zou, A., Wang, Z., Carlini, N., Nasr, M., Kolter, J. Z., & Fredrikson, M. (2023). Universal and transferable adversarial attacks on aligned language models (arXiv:2307.15043). arXiv. https://doi.org/10.48550/arXiv.2307.15043
2. Wei, Alexander & Haghtalab, Nika & Steinhardt, Jacob. (2023). Jailbroken: How Does LLM Safety Training Fail?. https://doi.org/10.48550/arXiv.2307.02483.
3. Brundage, M., Avin, S., Wang, J., Belfield, H., Krueger, G., Hadfield, G., Khlaaf, H., Yang, J., Toner, H., Fong, R., Maharaj, T., Koh, P. W., Hooker, S., Leung, J., Trask, A., Bluemke, E., Lebensold, J., O'Keefe, C., Koren, M., ... Anderljung, M. (2020). Toward trustworthy AI development: Mechanisms for supporting verifiable claims (arXiv:2004.07213). arXiv. https://doi.org/10.48550/arXiv.2004.07213
4. Perez, E., Huang, S., Song, F., Cai, T., Ring, R., Aslanides, J., Glaese, A., McAleese, N., & Irving, G. (2022). Red teaming language models with language models (arXiv:2202.03286). arXiv. https://doi.org/10.48550/arXiv.2202.03286
5. Bommasani, R., Hudson, D. A., Adeli, E., Altman, R., Arora, S., von Arx, S., Bernstein, M. S., Bohg, J., Bosselut, A., Brunskill, E., Brynjolfsson, E., Buch, S., Card, D., Castellon, R., Chatterji, N., Chen, A., Creel, K., Davis, J. Q., Demszky, D., ... Liang, P. (2022). On the opportunities and risks of foundation models (arXiv:2108.07258). arXiv. https://doi.org/10.48550/arXiv.2108.07258
6. Comiter, M. (2019). Attacking artificial intelligence: AI's security vulnerability and what policymakers can do about it. Belfer Center for Science and International Affairs, Harvard Kennedy School. https://www.belfercenter.org/publication/AttackingAI

7. Papernot, Nicolas & McDaniel, Patrick & Sinha, Arunesh & Wellman, Michael. (2018). SoK: Security and Privacy in Machine Learning. 399-414. https://doi.org/10.1109/EuroSP.2018.00035.
8. Biggio, B., Nelson, B., & Laskov, P. (2013). Poisoning attacks against support vector machines (arXiv:1206.6389). arXiv. https://doi.org/10.48550/arXiv.1206.6389
9. Szegedy, C., Zaremba, W., Sutskever, I., Bruna, J., Erhan, D., Goodfellow, I., & Fergus, R. (2014). Intriguing properties of neural networks (arXiv:1312.6199). arXiv. https://doi.org/10.48550/arXiv.1312.6199
10. Tramèr, F., Zhang, F., Juels, A., Reiter, M. K., & Ristenpart, T. (2016). Stealing machine learning models via prediction APIs. En Proceedings of the 25th USENIX Security Symposium (USENIX Security 16) (pp. 601–618). USENIX Association. https://www.usenix.org/conference/usenixsecurity16/technical-sessions/presentation/tramer
11. Kumar, Aman & Shankar, Amit & Hollebeek, Linda D. & Behl, Abhishek & Lim, Weng Marc, 2025. "Generative artificial intelligence (GenAI) revolution: A deep dive into GenAI adoption," Journal of Business Research, Elsevier, vol. 189(C).
12. Papernot, N., McDaniel, P., Goodfellow, I., Jha, S., Celik, Z. B., & Swami, A. (2017). Practical black-box attacks against machine learning. En Proceedings of the 2017 ACM on Asia Conference on Computer and Communications Security (AsiaCCS '17) (pp. 506–519). Association for Computing Machinery. https://doi.org/10.1145/3052973.3053009
13. Orekondy, T., Schiele, B., & Fritz, M. (2019). Knockoff nets: Stealing functionality of black-box models. En Proceedings of the IEEE/CVF Conference on Computer Vision and Pattern Recognition (CVPR 2019) (pp. 4954–4963). IEEE. https://doi.org/10.1109/CVPR.2019.00509
14. Juuti, M., Szyller, S., Marchal, S., & Asokan, N. (2019). PRADA: Protecting against DNN model stealing attacks. En Proceedings of the 2019 IEEE European Symposium on Security and Privacy (EuroS&P 2019) (pp. 512–527). IEEE. https://doi.org/10.1109/EuroSP.2019.00042
15. Carlini, N., Liu, C., Erlingsson, Ú., Kos, J., & Song, D. (2020). *The Secret Sharer: Evaluating and Testing Unintended Memorization in Neural Networks*. USENIX Security '20, 267–284.
16. Steinhardt, J., Koh, P. W., & Liang, P. (2017). *Certified defenses for data poisoning attacks*. NIPS '17, 3517–3529.
17. Koh, P. W., Steinhardt, J., & Liang, P. (2021). Stronger data poisoning attacks break data sanitization defenses (arXiv:1811.00741). arXiv. https://doi.org/10.48550/arXiv.1811.00741
18. Gu, T., Dolan-Gavitt, B., & Garg, S. (2017). *BadNets: Identifying vulnerabilities in the machine learning model supply chain*. arXiv preprint arXiv:1708.06733.
19. Bagdasaryan, E., Veit, A., Hua, Y., Estrin, D. & Shmatikov, V.. (2020). How To Backdoor Federated Learning. *Proceedings of the Twenty Third International Conference on Artificial Intelligence and Statistics*, in *Proceedings of Machine Learning Research* 108:2938-2948 Available from https://proceedings.mlr.press/v108/bagdasaryan20a.html
20. Carlini, N., Jagielski, M., Choquette-Choo, C. A., Paleka, D., Pearce, W., Anderson, H., Terzis, A., Thomas, K., & Tramèr, F. (2024). Poisoning web-scale training datasets is practical (arXiv:2302.10149). arXiv. https://doi.org/10.48550/arXiv.2302.10149
21. IEEE Standard for Fail-Safe Design of Autonomous and Semi-Autonomous Systems, StdP7009TM-2024, IEEE Reliability Society and Computer Society, May2024. [Online]. Available: IEEE Get Program. Accessed: Jul.2025.
22. Goodfellow, I. J., Shlens, J., & Szegedy, C. (2015). Explaining and harnessing adversarial examples. *arXiv preprint* arXiv:1412.6572.
23. Madry, A., Makelov, A., Schmidt, L., Tsipras, D., & Vladu, A. (2018). Towards deep learning models resistant to adversarial attacks. In *International Conference on Learning Representations (ICLR)*.
24. Dwork, C., & Ilvento, C. (2016). Algorithmic fairness: A primer. Communications of the ACM, 59(2), 33–35. https://doi.org/10.1145/2879679

25. Abadi, M., Chu, A., Goodfellow, I., McMahan, H. B., Mironov, I., Talwar, K., & Zhang, L. (2016). Deep learning with differential privacy. In *Proceedings of the 2016 ACM SIGSAC Conference on Computer and Communications Security* (pp. 308–318).
26. Liu, H., Wang, Y., Fan, W., Liu, X., Li, Y., Jain, S., Liu, Y., Jain, A. K., & Tang, J. (2021). Trustworthy AI: A computational perspective (arXiv:2107.06641). arXiv. https://doi.org/10.48550/arXiv.2107.06641
27. Katz, G., Barrett, C., Dill, D., Julian, K., & Kochenderfer, M. (2017). Reluplex: An efficient SMT solver for verifying deep neural networks (arXiv:1702.01135). arXiv. https://doi.org/10.48550/arXiv.1702.01135
28. Kattnig, M., Angerschmid, A., Reichel, T., & Kern, R. (2024). Assessing trustworthy AI: Technical and legal perspectives of fairness in AI. Computer Law & Security Review, 55, Article 106053. https://doi.org/10.1016/j.clsr.2024.106053

6 Malicious Uses of AI: Dual-Use Risks and Negative Requirements

6.1 Introduction to Dual-Use Concepts

The term dual-use refers to technologies that can be employed for both beneficial and harmful purposes. While originally rooted in the context of military and civilian applications—such as nuclear technology used for energy or for weapons—the concept has been broadened to include any innovation with the potential to serve conflicting goals. A single system or tool may advance medicine, education, or security, while simultaneously being misused to deceive, surveil, or harm. In the field of artificial intelligence (AI), dual-use refers to systems that, although developed for legitimate or even socially desirable purposes, can be repurposed—intentionally or inadvertently—for malicious ends. For example, a language model created to improve automated translation can also be manipulated to generate disinformation or hate speech at scale. Similarly, facial recognition tools intended for secure access control may be repurposed for population surveillance in repressive regimes.

Dual-use challenges are especially pressing in AI due to the increasing openness of the research community, the modularity of tools, and the limited control developers may have over how their systems are applied in the real world. Unlike traditional physical technologies, which often require significant resources to repurpose, many AI models can be adapted with minimal effort, requiring only new data inputs or minor adjustments to the code. This flexibility underscores the urgency of developing governance mechanisms that anticipate and address such risks early in the design process. This dual-use nature does not imply inherent malice in the technology itself, but rather highlights the importance of context, intention, and governance. The table below illustrates this contrast by presenting examples of AI applications alongside their intended (legitimate) purposes and potential misuse scenarios. Recognizing this duality is essential for anticipating ethical risks, designing safeguards, and fostering responsible innovation (Table 6.1).

R. Andrade et al., *Building Ethical and Secure AI*, Synthesis Lectures on Computer Science,
https://doi.org/10.1007/978-3-032-25789-5_6

Table 6.1 Examples of dual-use AI technologies and their contrasting purposes

AI technology	Intended use (Legitimate purpose)	Potential misuse (Malicious purpose)
Pregnancy risk prediction models	Assist physicians in detecting early signs of maternal-fetal complications and improving prenatal care	Manipulate outcomes to deny insurance coverage or target vulnerable groups through biased data
Medical diagnostic systems	Provide timely and personalized diagnoses, especially in under-resourced areas	Extract private medical records or infer patient identities through model exploitation
AI-powered hiring tools	Automate candidate pre-screening to improve efficiency and reduce administrative bias	Encode or amplify discriminatory patterns, or manipulate outcomes through adversarial inputs
Credit scoring algorithms	Offer more accurate assessments for loan approval and financial services	Discriminate based on socioeconomic or demographic features; enable strategic gaming of the scoring system
Autonomous surveillance systems	Monitor public spaces for safety and crowd management	Facilitate mass surveillance, social control, or targeting of political dissidents
Large Language Models (LLMs)	Assist users in writing, summarizing, and information retrieval across disciplines	Generate disinformation, phishing emails, or toxic content at scale

The dilemmas posed by dual-use are not new. In biotechnology, for example, research into genetic engineering has advanced life-saving treatments and agricultural innovations, yet also raised concerns about bio-weapons and synthetic pathogens. Organizations such as the World Health Organization and the Biological Weapons Convention have long worked to manage the challenges that arise when scientific advancements carry the potential for both benefit and harm. In areas such as biotechnology, efforts to support innovation often go hand in hand with the need to establish boundaries that reduce the risk of misuse. This balancing act requires not only technical understanding but also ongoing dialogue between scientists, policymakers, and the public. In cryptography, dual-use concerns have long influenced policy debates. Encryption technologies were originally developed to ensure the confidentiality of communications and to protect personal and sensitive information. Over time, they became a key part of everyday digital interactions—from online banking to private messaging. However, the same tools that help individuals safeguard their privacy have also been used by criminal groups and authoritarian governments to hide unlawful activity and avoid detection. This dual nature has sparked ongoing debate. On one side, there is the concern for public safety and the need to investigate serious crimes. On the other hand, there is the importance of maintaining secure systems that people and institutions can rely on. In some cases, governments have called for the creation of access points—often referred to as backdoors—that would allow authorities to bypass encryption when necessary. Yet, such proposals have raised difficult questions about who controls access, how systems remain secure, and whether weakening protections for some could end up affecting everyone. Rather than offering a simple solution, the debate over encryption shows how technology can serve different purposes depending on how it is used and by whom. It also reminds us that policy decisions in this area often involve trade-offs that affect security, rights, and the balance of power in society.

One of the most well-known examples of a technology with far-reaching consequences is nuclear fission. Initially understood as a scientific breakthrough in the early twentieth century, it soon gave rise to two distinct paths: the generation of electricity and the development of weapons. The Manhattan Project marked a turning point, showing how a research effort could quickly shift toward military goals once governments recognized its potential. In the years that followed, states and international organizations worked to set limits. Treaties were signed, oversight mechanisms were created, and monitoring systems were put in place. These efforts didn't eliminate risk, but they reflected a shared recognition that some forms of knowledge and technology require coordinated oversight.

Similar issues are now emerging in the field of artificial intelligence. Like biotechnology, cryptography, and nuclear fission, AI involves systems that can be applied in many settings, with effects that are difficult to predict in advance. However, artificial intelligence presents a set of challenges that differ from those found in earlier fields, such as biotechnology or nuclear science. One of its defining features is its flexibility. General-purpose models, especially those built on large-scale architectures, can be adapted for a wide range of tasks with relatively minor adjustments. A system initially trained to support scientific work, for example, can just as easily be used to generate convincing but inaccurate content. This capacity to shift from one purpose to another, often without much friction, makes it harder to anticipate how these tools might be used once they are publicly available. Another feature that sets AI apart is how easily it can be scaled. Once a model is built, it can be copied, embedded in applications, and distributed almost instantly. There is no need to transport physical materials or rely on complex infrastructure. A program developed in one country can be accessed and run elsewhere in minutes. This kind of reach, combined with low barriers to replication, makes it difficult to contain harmful uses once they begin to circulate. So questions arise about how to guide development in ways that are responsible and responsive to changing conditions.

The duality makes AI a prototypical example of the dual-use dilemma:

- Miller, a single technological advance may lead to both highly beneficial and ethically questionable outcomes [1]. In more depth, Miller highlights the dual-use dilemma as the ethical tension wherein a single scientific advance can serve both beneficial and harmful purposes. For instance, research on the mousepox virus could help control pests but also enable bioterrorism by creating vaccine-resistant pathogens.

- Collingridge Dilemma (1980): early-stage interventions in AI development are easier to implement but lack foresight, whereas late-stage interventions—when societal impacts become apparent—are significantly harder to execute [2].

Although Miller & Selgelid's "dual-use dilemma" and Collingridge's control dilemma were formulated for biotechnology and general technology studies, their analytical core adapts seamlessly to contemporary AI. In modern machine learning practice, general-purpose architectures—large language models, diffusion networks, or vision transformers—are inherently flexible artefacts whose consequences cannot be exhaustively predicted at design time, mirroring Collingridge's insight that early steering is easy but foresight is low, while late intervention is difficult despite high visibility of harms. Similarly, the dual-use dilemma now manifests in the ease with which a single codebase can pivot from medical image segmentation to pervasive biometric surveillance or from protein-folding prediction to synthetic-pathogen design. Recent scholarship on "foundational models" (Bommasani et al. [3]) and "AI security red teaming" (Brundage et al. [4]) explicitly reframes these classic dilemmas for AI, arguing that proactive governance—e.g., capability audits, risk-adjusted release strategies, and formal negative requirements—operationalizes the twin imperatives of anticipatory harm prevention and innovation preservation that the original theories identified.

Thus, AI systems do not possess intrinsic moral valence, but they carry embedded values and affordances depending on how, where, and by whom they are trained and deployed. Recognizing this dual-use nature is essential for designing AI governance frameworks that balance innovation with restraint. The ability to repurpose AI systems for malicious intent—whether by design, by omission, or by adversarial misuse—raises ethical concerns that must be addressed not only through governance but through engineering.

- Can all harmful behaviors be anticipated and formalized?
- Does formalization dilute the normative meaning of ethics?
- What happens when constraints conflict with each other?

In the pursuit of operationalizing ethics within AI systems, formal constraints and negative requirements have emerged as essential instruments for mitigating dual-use risks and preventing misuse. However, the act of translating normative concerns—such as fairness, dignity, or autonomy—into formal specifications introduces epistemic and ethical tensions. While technical formalism offers precision and enforceability, it may simultaneously obscure contextual nuance, moral ambiguity, and the fluid nature of human values. These tensions become especially salient when we attempt to preemptively constrain all potential harms, knowing that real-world scenarios are inherently open-ended and adversarial behavior evolves. As we deepen the integration of ethics into AI development, it becomes crucial to interrogate the limitations and paradoxes of formalization itself.

The identification and formalization of *constraints* constitute a foundational axis in requirements engineering for AI-enabled systems, as they define the *boundaries of permissible behavior* that must never be crossed under any operational context. Scholars have emphasized that, in the absence of explicitly encoded constraints, data-driven optimization processes can produce unintended consequences that infringe upon fundamental rights or erode public trust [5]. Building on the normative taxonomy proposed by Mittelstadt et al. [6] and extended by Yeung [7], constraints can be categorized based on their normative source—legal, ethical, operational, or socio-cultural. Table 6.2 synthesizes these types, offering representative examples and suitable formalization techniques, thus providing a conceptual and technical bridge between normative theory and formal verification practices in AI.

To confront these challenges, the chapter introduces the concept of *negative requirements*—formalized prohibitions and constraints that explicitly delineate what an AI system must never do. Drawing from formal methods, ethics of technology, and security policy, it proposes an interdisciplinary framework to detect, anticipate, and contain malicious behaviors. Rather than relying solely on reactive mitigation, it advocates for a design philosophy grounded in proactive restriction, dual-use foresight, and socio-technical governance.

Table 6.2 Types of constraints in AI-enabled systems

Constraint type	Description	Examples	Formalization techniques
Legal constraints	Constraints derived from formal laws, regulations, and compliance mandates	GDPR (EU), HIPAA (USA), Equal Credit Opportunity Act (USA), EU AI act	First-order logic (FOL), Linear Temporal Logic (LTL), runtime enforcement
Ethical constraints	Based on moral philosophy and institutional ethics principles	Do no harm, non-discrimination, autonomy, beneficence	Deontic logic, temporal logic (LTL/CTL), weighted rules
Operational constraints	Arise from performance, availability, and physical/systemic limitations	Max 80% CPU usage, action deadlines, sensor accuracy	Signal Temporal Logic (STL), system contracts, monitoring policies
Domain-specific constraints	Unique to the application context and expert-driven norms	No engagement with civilians (military), do not override surgeon decisions (medical AI)	Ontological rule systems, hybrid automata, domain-specific models
Social/Cultural constraints	Reflect societal norms, taboos, and user sensitivities	No gender inference from name, avoid religious recommendations	NLP filters, probabilistic rules, contextual soft constraints

6.2 Examples of Malicious Applications

Artificial intelligence has been exploited in multiple domains for malicious purposes, demonstrating its dual-use nature. Notable examples include:

- **Deepfakes and disinformation**: AI-generated synthetic media has been used to manipulate political discourse, such as falsified videos during the 2020 U.S. election campaigns and propaganda in conflict regions [8].
- **Automated cyberattacks**: Machine learning enhances phishing campaigns by personalizing messages at scale and bypassing traditional detection systems [9].
- **AI for fraud:** Voice-cloning AI has been used in corporate scams, such as the 2019 case where attackers mimicked a CEO's voice to authorize a fraudulent transfer exceeding $240,000.
- **Weaponized autonomous systems**: Lethal autonomous drones, as reported in the Libyan conflict (2020), allegedly operated without direct human oversight [10].

Deepfake in Political Manipulation
In 2023, an AI-generated video depicting a European political leader making inflammatory remarks went viral before being debunked. The deepfake sparked unrest and polarized public opinion.

- How should regulators address the malicious use of generative AI in democratic contexts?
- Should AI developers be held accountable for how their models are misused?

Autonomous AI agents executing cyber-espionage without human intervention, AI manipulating global financial systems to trigger economic destabilization, or autonomous military swarms escalating armed conflicts beyond human control.

6.3 Emerging Risks and Escalation

The risks posed by malicious AI are not static; they evolve as systems grow more capable and autonomous [11].

- **Escalation dynamics**: Minor incidents (e.g., localized disinformation) can scale into societal disruptions (e.g., widespread polarization, civil unrest).
- **Emerging risks**: As AI approaches artificial general intelligence (AGI), risks expand to include autonomous decision-making beyond human comprehension, cyber-physical attacks on critical infrastructure, and escalation of AI-driven arms races.

- **Compound threats**: Integration of AI with other emerging technologies (e.g., biotechnology, quantum computing) could amplify cascading risks.

Ethical reflection: Should global AI development be slowed to prevent escalation, or should robust governance mechanisms be prioritized to mitigate emerging threats?

6.4 Limitations of Current Governance Mechanisms

Despite numerous AI governance initiatives, substantial gaps remain [12, 13]:

- **Fragmentation**: Frameworks like the OECD AI Principles (2019) and the EU AI Act (2024) lack global enforceability and consistent adoption.
- **Reactive regulation**: Most mechanisms address known harms, failing to anticipate novel, rapidly emerging threats.
- **Jurisdictional challenges**: Malicious AI often transcends borders, but no binding international framework exists to address cross-border accountability.
- **Lack of enforcement**: Many principles remain voluntary, with insufficient oversight or sanctions for non-compliance.

Governance Gaps in AI Weapons *Autonomous drones are deployed in conflict zones by a private contractor, bypassing international humanitarian law. No international authority holds the contractor accountable.*

- Should the UN establish a dedicated AI oversight body?
- How can voluntary principles be transformed into enforceable regulations?

6.5 Typology of Malicious Applications

As Artificial Intelligence systems become increasingly integrated into critical infrastructure, software products, and decision-making processes, their misuse poses serious risks. Malicious applications of AI involve not only traditional hacking methods but also new and sophisticated techniques that leverage AI itself to evade, deceive, and exploit. Below is a typology outlining the major forms of malicious AI applications currently identified by researchers and security practitioners. Table 6.3 provides an overview of key categories associated with the malicious use of artificial intelligence. Each row highlights a specific type

Table 6.3 Examples of typology of malicious applications of AI

Category	Example	Main risk
Adversarial attacks	Subtle image perturbations that mislead AI classifiers	Incorrect automated decisions
Data poisoning	Manipulated training data that biases model behavior	Compromised or sabotaged AI models
Model extraction and inversion	Reconstructing a model via API queries or recovering training data	Loss of intellectual property and privacy breaches
Generative AI misuse	Deepfakes, fake news, and AI-generated phishing content	Fraud, misinformation, and reputational damage
Embedded malicious models (Backdoors)	Hidden triggers that cause the model to behave maliciously	Unauthorized control over AI behavior
AI-powered malware	Malware that learns and adapts in real time to evade detection	Dynamic evasion of cybersecurity defenses
Physical system manipulation	GPS spoofing or adversarial road signs misleading autonomous vehicles	Physical harm and critical system failure
Malicious bias injection	Intentional skewing of data to produce discriminatory outcomes	Social injustice and erosion of fairness

of threat, accompanied by a representative example and its principal associated risk. This typology serves as a foundational reference for understanding how AI technologies can be exploited across different domains, from cybersecurity to physical systems and social integrity.

6.5.1 Adversarial Attacks

Adversarial attacks exploit vulnerabilities in machine learning models by introducing subtle, often imperceptible changes to input data. These perturbations can mislead AI systems into making incorrect decisions—for example, causing an image classifier to identify a stop sign as a speed limit sign. This type of attack is particularly concerning in high-stakes environments such as autonomous vehicles, facial recognition systems, or malware detection engines [14].

Adversarial perturbations involve subtle, often imperceptible changes to input data—such as an image—that cause the model to misclassify it. A classic example is altering a stop sign in such a way that an autonomous vehicle misinterprets it as a speed limit sign. Though the changes may be nearly invisible to humans, they exploit the high sensitivity of neural networks to pixel-level modifications. These attacks pose critical risks to safety in computer vision systems used in self-driving cars, surveillance, and healthcare diagnostics.

Evasion attacks, on the other hand, are crafted to avoid detection by AI-based classifiers. In cybersecurity contexts, attackers may slightly modify malicious files so they are no longer flagged as threats by an AI-powered antivirus or intrusion detection system. These attacks operate during the model's inference phase and are particularly threatening in domains that rely on real-time or automated decision-making.

Data poisoning attacks target the training phase of machine learning. By injecting manipulated data into the training set, attackers can bias the model's learning process or introduce hidden vulnerabilities. This can result in a model that either performs poorly on certain tasks or behaves maliciously when exposed to specific triggers. Poisoning is especially dangerous in settings where training data is collected automatically or from untrusted sources, such as crowdsourced datasets, open web scraping, or continuous learning environments. Attackers can exploit this openness by submitting seemingly valid examples that distort statistical patterns the model is trying to learn. Even a small fraction of poisoned data—sometimes less than 1%—can be enough to degrade performance or embed undetectable vulnerabilities. There are also targeted vs. indiscriminate poisoning strategies. Targeted poisoning aims to affect model behavior on specific inputs or classes, while indiscriminate poisoning seeks to reduce overall model accuracy or increase its error rate. These attacks are particularly effective against deep neural networks due to their overfitting tendencies and reliance on large, diverse datasets. Defending against data poisoning requires robust data validation pipelines, provenance tracking, anomaly detection techniques, and in some cases, robust training methods such as differential privacy or certified defenses. As AI adoption grows, so too does the risk that its learning processes can be silently subverted before deployment, making data poisoning one of the most urgent threats in machine learning security. Table 6.4 offers a practical overview of how data poisoning attacks can differ in nature and execution. Rather than treating them as a single type of threat, it breaks them down by their purpose, when they occur, how much the attacker knows, the way poisoned data is introduced, and how widespread the manipulation is. This helps illustrate the many ways in which these attacks can be carried out—and why detecting them isn't always straightforward.

Together, these three forms of adversarial attacks challenge the integrity, reliability, and trustworthiness of AI systems. They highlight the need for robust defenses such as adversarial training, anomaly detection, and validation of training-data sources.

6.5.2 Model Extraction and Inversion

Model extraction and inversion attacks focus on exploiting access to trained AI models—particularly those exposed via public or commercial APIs—to either replicate their internal workings or reveal sensitive information from their training data. These attacks compromise

Table 6.4 Subclassification of data poisoning attacks in machine learning

Classification criterion	Subcategories and description
Attack objective	**Targeted**: Affects specific inputs or classes (e.g., misclassify one person) **Indiscriminate**: Degrades overall model performance across many inputs
Attack timing	**Pre-training**: Poisoning occurs before the model is trained, often via untrusted datasets **Online / Continual Learning**: Poisoning occurs during ongoing updates or live data ingestion
Attacker's knowledge	**White-box**: Full access to model structure and training data, enabling optimized poisoning **Black-box**: Limited knowledge, usually only access to data pipeline or input interface
Injection strategy	**Label flipping**: Mislabeling existing examples to confuse the model **Feature Manipulation**: Crafting inputs with deceptive but valid features. **Backdoor injection**: Embedding hidden triggers to activate misbehavior at inference time
Poisoning scale	**High-scale**: Large portion of the dataset is poisoned—easier to detect **Low-scale/Clean-label**: Few poisoned examples that appear benign—harder to detect

the confidentiality and proprietary value of AI systems, and in some cases, they can also lead to serious privacy violations [10, 15, 21].

Model extraction Also known as model stealing, occurs when an attacker repeatedly queries a machine learning model—primarily through a deployed API—and uses the input-output pairs to reconstruct a functionally equivalent surrogate model. This surrogate can often perform just as well as the original. In some cases, it may even reveal insights into the architecture, hyperparameters, or training data used to create the original model. This type of attack poses a significant threat to companies offering Machine Learning-as-a-Service (MLaaS), as it enables attackers to circumvent licensing, lower R&D expenses, and potentially integrate malicious modifications into replicated systems.

Model Inversion In parallel, model inversion attacks aim to recover private or sensitive information from a trained model. By analyzing how the model responds to specific inputs, attackers can infer characteristics of the underlying training data or even reconstruct original data samples. For instance, a model trained for facial recognition might inadvertently allow an attacker to reconstruct facial images of individuals from its training set. This is especially problematic in healthcare, biometrics, and other fields where models are trained on personally identifiable or regulated data. These attacks are particularly potent against models that are overfit, highly expressive, or trained with limited regularization. Moreover, many AI models unintentionally memorize rare or outlier data points from their training sets, making them especially vulnerable to inversion. Combined, model stealing and inversion highlight the importance of not just protecting data pipelines but also securing the model itself after deployment. Mitigation strategies include limiting API access through rate limiting, query monitoring, watermarking model outputs, adding differential privacy during training, and using techniques like knowledge distillation to reduce the information leakage of the model. As AI models become more accessible through cloud platforms and APIs, ensuring their confidentiality and robustness against extraction and inversion becomes a critical component of AI security governance.

6.5.3 Generative AI Misuse

The rapid advancement of generative artificial intelligence has unlocked extraordinary creative potential, but it has also introduced powerful tools for deception, manipulation, and harm. When these technologies are misused, the consequences are not merely technical—they impact trust, public discourse, and personal safety. The following are three prominent forms of malicious use of generative AI that have already shown tangible effects across social, political, and economic domains [16].

Deepfakes and Synthetic Media

AI-powered generative models, such as GANs or diffusion transformers, have been weaponized to produce disinformation campaigns and reputational attacks. The lack of verifiable provenance mechanisms complicates accountability. Deepfakes are generated using advanced generative models—originally GANs, now increasingly replaced by diffusion-based models like Stable Diffusion or DALL-E 3. These models learn joint distributions over data modalities, allowing for high-fidelity synthesis of images and audio. The core innovation lies in *latent controllability*, which allows a user to guide the output generation process to mimic identities or behaviors with minimal input (Table 6.5).

Fake news using large language models. These LLMs, capable of producing fluent and authoritative-sounding text, can generate false narratives on virtually any topic. Malicious actors exploit this ability to flood online spaces with coordinated disinformation, whether to influence elections, provoke social unrest, or undermine trust in institutions. The scale at which this can occur—paired with the personalization possible through AI—amplifies its reach and makes fact-checking reactive and insufficient. Unlike traditional propaganda, AI-generated misinformation can adapt to different audiences and mimic credible sources, making it more insidious and harder to detect.

Phishing attacks have taken on a far more convincing and dangerous form thanks to generative AI. What used to be clumsy, poorly written scam emails can now appear as polished, professional messages that seem entirely legitimate. Attackers no longer need to

Table 6.5 Illustrative threat vectors of deepfakes

Vector	Malicious objective	Example	Impact layer
Political disinformation	Fabricated speeches or surrenders	"Deepfake zelensky" video (2022)	National morale, elections
Reputational harm	Non-consensual pornography	Telegram harassment (2020)	Psychological, professional
Financial fraud	CEO impersonation via voice cloning	UK $240K scam (2019)	Corporate loss, trust erosion
Security evasion	Bypass face recognition systems	GAN + mask prototypes	Border control, surveillance

rely on guesswork—they can create emails that reflect the tone, style, and urgency of real workplace communication. These messages might look like a note from your manager, a request from a colleague, or a routine system alert, but with a malicious intent hidden beneath their familiar surface. Because AI makes it easy to generate these at scale and with precision, attackers can launch widespread phishing campaigns with little effort, while making each message feel personal and credible. The result is a growing risk that even vigilant individuals may be caught off guard.

6.5.4 Embedded Malicious Models (Backdoors)

Artificial intelligence models, especially those obtained from third parties or open repositories, can sometimes harbor hidden behaviors—intentional and malicious—that remain dormant until activated by a specific signal. These covert mechanisms, commonly known as backdoors, are carefully embedded during the training process or model assembly. To the naked eye and under regular operation, the model performs its task as expected. However, once a particular trigger is introduced—often subtle and crafted to escape detection—the model shifts its behavior in a way that serves the attacker's interests. This type of manipulation poses a serious risk, particularly in systems responsible for authentication, security enforcement, or automated decision-making [17–19].

Input-based backdoor, where the model responds abnormally only when presented with a specific input pattern or token. For example, in an image classification system, a model might correctly label most objects unless a tiny sticker or symbol is present, at which point it deliberately misclassifies the image. These triggers can be visual, textual, or data-driven, and are designed to be inconspicuous enough to avoid raising alarms during testing or deployment. This makes them ideal for use in systems like facial recognition or surveillance, where a single misclassification can allow unauthorized individuals to slip through undetected.

Contextual or conditional backdoor, which activates not through a fixed signal, but under certain conditions. These could include time-based triggers (e.g., the model misbehaves only during specific hours), user-specific scenarios (e.g., only for particular accounts), or a combination of input features that collectively act as a switch. Such attacks are more challenging to identify because the malicious behavior is embedded in logic rather than a static cue, making traditional input sanitization or filtering ineffective. This form of manipulation is particularly worrisome in dynamic environments like recommendation systems or autonomous decision-making platforms, where triggers can be deeply intertwined with user behavior.

Semantic backdoor, where the poisoned behavior mimics legitimate reasoning. For instance, a language model might prioritize or suppress certain types of content when given politically charged phrases or respond differently to questions based on slight wording changes. These backdoors often go unnoticed because their outputs can be defended as subjective or ambiguous. However, in practice, they offer a way to systematically skew outcomes, moderate content in biased ways, or suppress certain viewpoints under the guise of regular operation.

What makes embedded backdoors especially dangerous is that their presence is hard to prove without complete control over the model's training data and process—an increasingly rare condition as models grow in size and complexity. Even exhaustive testing can fail to uncover these traps if the trigger conditions are well-crafted. As such, they represent a profound challenge not only for cybersecurity but for the integrity and trustworthiness of AI systems as a whole.

6.5.5 AI-Powered Malware

The integration of artificial intelligence into malware has opened a new frontier of adaptability and stealth in digital threats. Unlike conventional malicious software, AI-enhanced malware does not follow static rules or signatures—it observes, learns, and refines its behavior based on the environment in which it operates. This dynamic nature makes it significantly harder for traditional security systems to anticipate or block its actions [20, 21].

Adaptive Evasion Malware. These threats monitor the behavior of security tools and adjust their strategies accordingly. For example, they may detect if they are being executed in a sandboxed environment—a common technique for malware analysis—and alter their behavior to appear benign, only activating once deployed on a real machine. This creates a cat-and-mouse dynamic in which the malware continuously evolves to outpace detection.

Decision-optimizing malware, which uses reinforcement learning or similar methods to select the most effective attack vectors. Rather than relying on predefined commands, these systems evaluate multiple options and pursue the ones with the highest chance of success, whether it be lateral movement across a network, privilege escalation, or data exfiltration. This intelligent decision-making makes such attacks more targeted and efficient.

Autonomous malicious bots, which use AI to perform harmful tasks with minimal oversight. These bots can carry out large-scale fraud operations, conduct automated scraping of protected data, or orchestrate denial-of-service attacks that respond in real time to defensive measures. Their ability to operate continuously and learn from failed attempts makes them remarkably resilient and difficult to suppress.

6.5.6 Physical System Manipulation

As artificial intelligence takes on greater responsibility in physical systems—drones, autonomous vehicles, industrial robots—new vulnerabilities have emerged that exploit the interface between the digital and physical worlds. These attacks do not target the AI code directly, but instead manipulate the information the system receives from its sensors, leading it to make dangerously flawed decisions.

Sensor spoofing is a technique where attackers deceive an AI system by feeding it false signals from its environment. Instead of hacking into the code directly, they tamper with what the system sees or senses, like altering GPS data, faking radar echoes, or interfering with camera input. Take an autonomous vehicle, for example: if it's misled into believing it's on a clear, open road when it's approaching an intersection or obstacle, the results could be catastrophic. What makes this type of attack particularly dangerous is how subtle it can be. The system continues operating as if everything is normal, unaware that it's responding to false information—until a critical error occurs.

Adversarial input manipulation, where visual or audio cues are altered just enough to confuse the system. An adversary might place carefully designed stickers on a traffic sign that cause a machine vision algorithm to misinterpret them, potentially making a vehicle accelerate when it should stop. These attacks exploit the model's sensitivity to small perturbations and are often inexpensive to carry out.

Environmental perturbation, in which the attacker influences the AI's operating context indirectly. This could involve manipulating lighting, acoustics, or surrounding physical layouts to degrade sensor performance or provoke system errors. Unlike direct hacks, these methods often leave no digital trace, making them particularly challenging to diagnose or attribute.

Model level influence, where the bias is injected not through the data, but by tweaking internal components like loss functions, class weights, or feature prioritization. These changes are often imperceptible to end users or even developers but can lead to consistent deviations in behavior that serve ideological, political, or financial goals. What makes malicious bias injection particularly dangerous is its plausibility. Unlike overt attacks, the outputs can always be rationalized or dismissed as model "limitations," allowing the manipulation to persist unchallenged. Detecting and mitigating such influence requires rigorous scrutiny of data provenance, transparency in model training processes, and, in some cases, third-party audits to safeguard against ethical violations.

6.6 Negative Requirements in AI Design

One of the most pressing issues is the lack of *verifiable provenance*. Metadata manipulation, recompression artifacts, and lack of cryptographic binding allow bad actors to deny authenticity or claim plausible deniability. This leads to what is known as the *liar's dividend*, where even truthful recordings can be discredited as fake.

Solutions span technical and governance layers:

- **Signal-level forensics**: GAN fingerprinting, PRNU analysis, and frequency-based anomaly detection are used to detect synthetic origins.
- **Provenance protocols**: The C2PA standard enables cryptographic signing of edits and origins. Watermarking-by-construction embeds identifiers at the model output.
- **Regulatory measures**: The EU AI Act mandates disclosure for synthetic content. China requires explicit labeling under its 2023 regulations.
- **Platform governance**: Prompt filtering, usage throttling, and content scoring are increasingly adopted in generative model APIs.

In this chapter will transition from specification to elicitation: how to capture ethical and legal requirements under uncertainty using goal-driven and semi-formal methods.

References

1. Miller, S., & Selgelid, M. J. (2007). *Ethical and philosophical consideration of the dual-use dilemma in the biological sciences*. Science and Engineering Ethics, 13(4), 523–580. Springer. Retrieved from https://doi.org/10.1007/s11948-007-9043-4
2. Genus, Audley & Stirling, Andy, 2018. "Collingridge and the dilemma of control: Towards responsible and accountable innovation," Research Policy, Elsevier, vol. 47(1), pages 61-69.
3. Bommasani, R., Hudson, D., Adeli, E., Altman, R., Arora, S., Arx, S., Bernstein, M., Bohg, J., Bosselut, A., Brunskill, E., Brynjolfsson, E., Buch, S., Card, D., Castellon, R., Chatterji, N., Chen, A., Creel, K., Davis, J., Demszky, D., & Liang, P. (2021). On the Opportunities and Risks of Foundation Models. *arXiv preprint* arXiv:2108.07258. https://doi.org/10.48550/arXiv.2108.07258
4. OpenAI. (2024). Practices for Governing Agentic AI Systems. *OpenAI Research Report*. Retrieved from https://cdn.openai.com/papers/practices-for-governing-agentic-ai-systems.pdf
5. Floridi, L., Cowls, J., Beltrametti, M., Chatila, R., Chazerand, P., Dignum, V., et al.: AI4People—An Ethical Framework for a Good AI Society: Opportunities, Risks, Principles, and Recommendations. *Minds and Machines* **28**(4), 689–707 (2018)
6. Mittelstadt, B. (2019). Principles alone cannot guarantee ethical AI. *Nature Machine Intelligence*, 1(11), 501–507.
7. Yeung, K. (2020). Recommendation of the Council on Artificial Intelligence (OECD). *International Legal Materials*, 59, 27–34. https://doi.org/10.1017/ilm.2020.5
8. Fandiño López, E. (2024). The risks of deepfakes for democracy and the prospects for regulation. Resistances. Journal of the Philosophy of History, 5(10), e240167. https://doi.org/10.46652/resistances.v5i10.167

9. European Union Agency for Law Enforcement Cooperation (Europol). (2023). Internet Organised Crime Threat Assessment (IOCTA) 2023. Publications Office of the European Union.
10. Dibbo, S. V. (2023, July). *Sok: Model inversion attack landscape: Taxonomy, challenges, and future roadmap*. In 2023 IEEE 36th Computer Security Foundations Symposium (CSF) (pp. 439-456). IEEE.
11. Bostrom, N. (2014). *Superintelligence: Paths, Dangers, Strategies*. Oxford University Press.
12. Future of Life Institute. (2024). EU Artificial Intelligence Act: Up-to-date developments and analyses of the EU AI Act. https://artificialintelligenceact.eu/
13. OECD. (2019). *OECD Principles on Artificial Intelligence*.
14. Xi, Hailong & Ru, Le & Jiwei, Tian & Lu, Bo & Hu, Shiguang & Wang, Wenfei. (2024). Adversarial Attacks: Key Challenges for Security Defense in the Age of Intelligence. 41-46. 10.1109/ICAIRC64177.2024.10900089.
15. Liu, R., Zhang, J., Lam, K. Y., Zhao, J., & Zhou, W. (2023, November). *SCME: A self-contrastive method for data-free and query-limited model extraction attack*. In International Conference on Neural Information Processing (pp. 370-382). Singapore: Springer Nature Singapore.
16. Marchal, N., Xu, R., Elasmar, R., Gabriel, I., Goldberg, B., & Isaac, W. (2024). *Generative AI misuse: A taxonomy of tactics and insights from real-world data*. arXiv preprint arXiv:2406.13843.
17. Peyrin, T., & Wang, H. (2020). The MALICIOUS framework: Embedding backdoors into tweakable block ciphers (IACR Cryptology ePrint Archive Report 2020/986). IACR Cryptology ePrint Archive. https://eprint.iacr.org/2020/986
18. Zhong, H., Liao, C., Squicciarini, A. C., Zhu, S., & Miller, D. (2020). Backdoor Embedding in Convolutional Neural Network Models via Invisible Perturbation. In CODASPY 2020 - Proceedings of the 10th ACM Conference on Data and Application Security and Privacy (pp. 97-108). (CODASPY 2020 - Proceedings of the 10th ACM Conference on Data and Application Security and Privacy). Association for Computing Machinery, Inc. https://doi.org/10.1145/3374664.3375751
19. Gong, Xueluan & Chen, Yanjiao & Yang, Wenbin & Huang, Huayang & Wang, Qian. (2023). B 3 : Backdoor Attacks Against Black-Box Machine Learning Models. ACM Transactions on Privacy and Security. 26. https://doi.org/10.1145/3605212.
20. Alanezi, M., & AL-Azzawi, R. M. A. (2024). *AI-Powered Cyber Threats: A Systematic Review*. Mesopotamian Journal of CyberSecurity, 4(3), 166-188.
21. Gong, X., Chen, Y., Yang, W., Mei, G., & Wang, Q. (2021). INVERSENET: Augmenting model extraction attacks with training data inversion. En Proceedings of the Thirtieth International Joint Conference on Artificial Intelligence (IJCAI-21) (pp. 2439–2447). International Joint Conferences on Artificial Intelligence Organization. https://doi.org/10.24963/ijcai.2021/336

Systemic Security, Resilience, and Multi-level Governance in AI

7

7.1 Security in AI-Enabled Systems

Security in AI-enabled systems cannot be reduced to traditional mechanisms such as access control, authentication, or data encryption. While these measures remain necessary, they are insufficient to address the complexity and dynamism of contemporary AI deployments. AI systems increasingly operate within socio-technical ecosystems, where technical components interact continuously with human actors, organizational processes, regulatory frameworks, and evolving threat landscapes. In such contexts, security emerges not as a static feature, but as an emergent system property shaped by interactions across multiple layers of the ecosystem.

This chapter conceptualizes security as a dynamic capability, emphasizing the system's ability to anticipate, withstand, adapt to, and recover from both adversarial attacks and unanticipated failures. Drawing on principles from resilience engineering, it highlights the importance of designing AI systems that can degrade gracefully, maintain core functionality under stress, and learn from disruptions.

7.2 Systemic Security, Resilience, and Multi-level Governance in AI

7.2.1 Systemic Security in AI

Systemic security refers not only to the protection of individual AI components, but to the emergent safety of the entire socio-technical ecosystem. AI systems operate within complex environments where technical vulnerabilities intertwine with social, legal, and organizational risks.

R. Andrade et al., *Building Ethical and Secure AI*, Synthesis Lectures on Computer Science,
https://doi.org/10.1007/978-3-032-25789-5_7

- **Ontological Security**: Security must be conceptualized beyond technical boundaries, incorporating threats such as adversarial attacks, data leakage, and algorithmic discrimination.
- **System-wide Vulnerabilities**: AI models that perform well in isolated environments may trigger cascading failures when embedded in critical infrastructures or global platforms.
- **Interdependencies**: Modern AI deployments often involve cloud infrastructure, APIs, IoT, and human feedback loops. A security flaw in one component may propagate throughout the system.

7.2.2 Resilience: Beyond Static Defense

Resilience emphasizes the ability of AI systems and institutions to withstand, adapt to, and recover from unexpected disruptions.

- **Robustness vs. Resilience**: Robust systems resist change; resilient systems recover from it. The latter is more suitable for dynamic and high-stakes AI environments.
- **Resilience Mechanisms**: Organizations must employ continuous model monitoring, fail-safe deactivation protocols, and post-deployment learning mechanisms such as retraining in response to socioeconomic shifts.
- **Example**: Credit scoring systems that adapt after financial crises to avoid perpetuating obsolete biases illustrate institutional resilience.

7.3 From Component Security to Systemic Assurance

7.3.1 Component Security: The Classical Paradigm

Traditional approaches to AI security emphasize the protection of discrete components such as algorithms, datasets, application interfaces, or sensors. This component-level perspective aims to ensure the classical security triad of **confidentiality, integrity, and availability (CIA)**.

- **Focus**: Protecting individual technical modules in isolation.
- **Common Practices**:
  - Adversarial training to defend against evasion attacks.
  - Input validation and anomaly detection.
  - Use of encryption, differential privacy, and secure enclaves.
  - Secure coding and DevSecOps methodologies.

- **Limitations**:
  - Ignores emergent risks arising from complex interactions.
  - Assumes that security guarantees persist across contexts.
  - Fails to address feedback loops, real-world deployment dynamics, and socio-technical entanglements.

7.3.2 The Shift to Systemic Assurance

Systemic assurance expands the security lens to encompass **interdependencies, emergent vulnerabilities, and socio-technical context**. This approach recognizes that even secure components can collectively produce unsafe outcomes.

- **Emergent Vulnerabilities**: Risks arise not from flawed parts, but from unanticipated interactions between parts.
- **Latent Risks**: Real-world deployment introduces complexities such as automation bias, distributional drift, and adversarial adaptation.
- **Contextual Variability**: Model behavior and risk profiles vary across environments, data populations, and regulatory regimes.

7.4 Defense in Depth in AI Systems: Multilayered Resilience for Complex Threat Landscapes

7.4.1 From Static Boundaries to Dynamic Attack Surfaces

Unlike conventional software systems, AI applications—particularly those involving Large Language Models (LLMs), reinforcement learning agents, or federated architectures—do not operate with clearly defined interfaces or deterministic behavior. As Brundage et al. emphasize in [3], AI systems must be defended "across the stack," from raw data ingestion and feature engineering to training pipelines, inference APIs, and feedback loops. This expands the classical notion of security perimeters and demands multi-layer resilience.

7.4.2 Institutional Guidance and International Standards

The *NIST AI Risk Management Framework (2023)* explicitly calls for a layered security architecture in AI, advocating for redundancy across:

- **Data Pipelines**: Protection against poisoning, exfiltration, and integrity loss.
- **Model Layers**: Encryption at rest, anomaly detection, and adversarial robustness.
- **APIs and Interfaces**: Rate-limiting, authentication, and schema validation.
- **Human Operators**: Role-based access control, decision audits, and training for secure AI deployment.

This aligns with *ISO/IEC 27001* [1] and the more recent *ISO/IEC 23894:2023* [2], which extends those principles to AI-specific risk management. These frameworks advocate for both horizontal defenses (multiple controls per layer) and vertical integration (linking design-time controls to runtime enforcement), ensuring traceability and policy continuity.

7.4.3 Strategic Objectives of Defense in Depth for AI

A robust Defense in Depth strategy for AI systems seeks to accomplish:

- **Containment of Failures**: Prevent cascading errors when a single layer is breached.
- **Redundancy and Fault Tolerance**: Multiple safeguards mitigate the same risk.
- **Proactive Threat Modeling**: Anticipating attack vectors unique to data and ML models.
- **Human-in-the-Loop (HITL) Resilience**: Incorporating oversight and override capabilities when automated layers become unreliable or compromised.

These principles are echoed in the IEEE's *Ethically Aligned Design* guidelines, which emphasize layered accountability, transparency, and control mechanisms throughout AI architectures.

7.4.4 Implementation Patterns

In order to operationalize systemic assurance within AI systems, it is essential to adopt a multi-layered defense strategy that addresses both adversarial and structural vulnerabilities. Techniques such as adversarial training and input sanitization at the data layer are foundational to enhance robustness against manipulation and perturbation-based attacks. However, resilience must extend beyond model-centric defenses to include infrastructural safeguards. Containerized and access-controlled serving environments—monitored through behavioral anomaly detection—are crucial for mitigating risks associated with unauthorized access and misuse. Furthermore, red-teaming exercises and simulated breaches on large language model (LLM) endpoints play a critical role in proactively identifying prompt injection and data exfiltration vulnerabilities, which are often overlooked in conventional testing pipelines. Complementing these technical interventions, end-to-end auditing frameworks provide traceability and accountability through mechanisms such as model lineage tracking, secure logging, and tamper-evident record-keeping using technologies like blockchain or secure enclaves. Collectively, these practices reinforce systemic assurance by embedding security and accountability throughout the AI lifecycle. In practice, this approach translates into:

- Adversarial training and input sanitization in the data layer.
- Access-controlled model serving environments, often containerized and monitored via behavioral anomaly detection.
- Red teaming and simulated breach exercises on LLM endpoints to identify prompt injection and extraction vulnerabilities.
- End-to-end auditing frameworks, using tools like model lineage tracking, secure logs, and tamper-evident records (e.g., via blockchain or secure enclaves).

7.5 Context-Aware Policies in AI Security

The principle of context-aware policies advocates that security and ethical governance mechanisms in AI systems must be dynamically aligned with the situational, demographic, and domain-specific characteristics of the application. This reflects a shift from rigid, one-size-fits-all security policies to adaptive frameworks that respond to contextual risk exposure and ethical sensitivities.

Floridi and Cowls introduce the AI4People framework, which identifies five foundational ethical principles for AI: beneficence, non-maleficence, autonomy, justice, and explicability. Crucially, they argue that the application of these principles must be modulated by context, especially when AI interacts with vulnerable populations or operates in high-stakes environments. For instance, the autonomy of users in a consumer chatbot scenario must be protected differently from autonomy in medical diagnosis or autonomous vehicles, which may involve life-critical decisions [3].

Amann et al. [4], in the domain of medical AI, demonstrate that algorithmic systems must not only be accurate but also context-sensitive. Clinical applications vary in urgency (e.g., emergency triage vs. routine screening), data availability, demographic factors, and diagnostic uncertainty. These variables affect the thresholds at which AI recommendations should be trusted or flagged for human oversight. From a security perspective, this necessitates policies that tune system confidence, audit trails, and escalation mechanisms based on contextual parameters.

IEEE's proposed standard P7009 on the governance of autonomous and intelligent systems similarly highlights the importance of contextual adaptation. It emphasizes that AI policies must incorporate socio-cultural values, legal constraints, and dynamic human preferences, ensuring that system behaviors respect contextually grounded expectations. This implies not only technical configurability but also governance architectures capable of monitoring and modifying policy enforcement in response to evolving conditions [5].

From a systems engineering standpoint, implementing context-aware security policies requires:

- **Context modeling**: Ontologies and metadata schemas to capture relevant situational variables (e.g., urgency, location, user vulnerability).
- **Policy orchestration engines**: Capable of adapting access control, audit logging, and inference boundaries.
- **Feedback mechanisms**: Enabling real-time adjustments based on user input or environmental changes.
- **Simulation and testing**: Evaluating policy robustness across diverse scenarios and adversarial contexts.

In summary, context-aware policies bridge the gap between abstract ethical principles and concrete operational decisions in AI systems. They embody a socio-technical approach to AI governance, acknowledging that trustworthiness, safety, and fairness are not static properties but dynamically situated obligations.

7.5.1 Interoperability Governance in Distributed AI Systems

The increasing deployment of AI in distributed and multi-agent ecosystems demands a robust framework for *interoperability governance*. This involves ensuring that autonomous systems, often developed by different vendors or functioning in disparate regulatory environments, can exchange data, interpret semantics consistently, and coordinate decision-making processes in a coherent and trustworthy manner.

From a theoretical standpoint, interoperability encompasses not just technical compatibility but also **semantic alignment**, **policy harmonization**, and **normative coherence**. As argued by Cihon et al. [6], the absence of standardized interfaces and common ontologies impairs the safe and effective functioning of AI systems, particularly in critical infrastructure domains such as healthcare, finance, and autonomous mobility.

Organizationally, the OECD [7] calls for the adoption of open standards and international regulatory alignment to promote responsible AI across borders. The ISO/IEC 42001 draft and the IEEE P7010 standard both stress the need for auditability, transparency, and legal interoperability between agents operating under varying jurisdictional constraints.

Technically, interoperability governance requires the implementation of modular architectures, clear interface contracts (APIs), shared data schemas, and mechanisms for conflict resolution and trust negotiation among agents. This is particularly relevant for multi-agent reinforcement learning (MARL) systems, federated learning networks, and cross-border AI supply chains, where misalignment can lead to the propagation of bias, errors, or even emergent unsafe behavior.

In sum, interoperability governance is not merely an engineering challenge, but a sociotechnical imperative. It mandates collaboration among regulators, standard bodies, developers, and civil society to co-design AI ecosystems that uphold shared values while remaining adaptive to local contexts.

7.5.2 Systemic Risk Scenarios

Systemic risks in artificial intelligence arise when localized failures scale into broader societal harms due to algorithmic opacity, interconnected infrastructures, and insufficient governance. One critical manifestation is undetected bias in predictive justice systems, which can lead to wrongful incarceration or disproportionate penalties for marginalized communities, as highlighted in reports by the AI Now Institute (2019) and documented in empirical studies of risk assessment tools like COMPAS. Poorly calibrated medical AI systems pose another systemic threat, particularly when trained on non-representative data, resulting in diagnostic disparities that compromise the right to health [4]. Recommendation algorithms that prioritize engagement metrics can unintentionally radicalize users, amplifying extremist content and fostering societal polarization—a concern emphasized in Brundage et al. [8] as an emergent security-ethics issue. Finally, unmonitored or corrupted AI models embedded in critical infrastructure (e.g., energy grids, emergency response) may autonomously propagate errors without human verification, leading to cascading failures. These examples underscore the need for proactive accountability frameworks, real-time monitoring, and multi-level oversight to mitigate AI-driven systemic risks across technical and social domains.

Table 7.1 summarizes representative examples of systemic risks in AI systems, highlighting scenarios where local algorithmic failures can scale into broader societal harms. These include undetected bias in criminal justice algorithms, miscalibrated medical diagnostic tools, recommendation engines that intensify social polarization, and unsupervised corrupted models operating within critical infrastructure. Each of these cases illustrates how inadequate governance, poor calibration, or a lack of human oversight can transform technical issues into ethical and social crises. The table reinforces the need for multi-layered risk mitigation strategies, spanning from model design and data governance to regulatory enforcement and institutional accountability.

Table 7.1 Examples of systemic risk in artificial intelligence

Examples of systemic risk in AI	Description
Undetected bias	Predictive justice models affecting liberty-related decisions
Poorly calibrated medical AI	Producing erroneous diagnoses in specific populations
Radicalizing recommendation algorithms	Contributing to social polarization or violence
Corrupted models without oversight	Automating erroneous decisions in critical infrastructure

- How do localized algorithmic errors escalate into systemic societal harms?
- What accountability mechanisms should be in place for AI systems operating in high-stakes domains such as justice, healthcare, or critical infrastructure?

7.5.3 Data Drift and Undetected Bias as a Source of Systemic Risk

One of the most critical sources of systemic risk in AI systems is the interaction between *data drift* and *undetected bias*. Data drift occurs when the statistical distribution of input data changes over time, which can misalign the model's learned parameters with its operational environment. If bias emerges or intensifies during this drift—particularly in sensitive applications such as criminal justice, hiring, or credit scoring—and remains undetected, the system may replicate or even exacerbate social inequalities at scale.

This dynamic is especially dangerous in feedback-loop scenarios. For example, biased decision-making in automated hiring systems or predictive policing can reinforce societal discrimination. As these systems produce outcomes based on historical patterns, they may collect data that validates and further trains the model on biased distributions—a phenomenon described as the *algorithmic feedback loop* [9, 10].

Systemically, this risk affects not just individuals but entire institutional structures. When decisions driven by AI systems consistently favor or penalize specific groups due to entrenched bias, it can lead to the erosion of public trust and legitimacy. This creates ethical and legal violations that propagate through interconnected societal systems, triggering crisis-level consequences. The EU AI Act explicitly categorizes such configurations—where biased decision-making can cause significant harm to fundamental rights—as *high-risk systems*. It mandates measures such as continuous bias monitoring, dataset documentation, and transparency obligations [11].

7.6 Resilience Engineering in AI Systems

Resilience in AI systems is increasingly recognized as a multidimensional property essential to ensuring operational continuity and trustworthiness in dynamic and high-risk environments. Theoretically, resilience encompasses the capacity of a system to anticipate potential disruptions, absorb their impact, adapt behaviorally or structurally, and recover functionality with minimal degradation in performance. According to Hollnagel et al. and Linkov et al., resilience in complex systems goes beyond traditional robustness and incorporates adaptive and proactive capabilities [12, 13]. Four interrelated dimensions typically characterize this quality:

Robustness refers to the system's ability to maintain performance under stress or uncertainty, such as adversarial attacks or sensor noise, as supported by theories of fault tolerance and robust optimization [14].

Redundancy, a principle borrowed from systems engineering, involves incorporating backup components or fallback procedures (e.g., human-in-the-loop) that can compensate for individual component failures, thereby increasing the system's fault tolerance.

Responsiveness entails the timely detection and mitigation of failure modes, often supported by anomaly detection mechanisms, monitoring tools, and feedback loops that align with principles of cybernetic control and adaptive systems [15].

Reconfigurability describes the system's capacity to modify its internal architecture or behavior dynamically, allowing for graceful degradation or switching to safe modes under duress—an idea rooted in control theory and adaptive system design [16]. Together, these elements frame resilience not merely as recovery, but as a proactive and systemic attribute that integrates technical, organizational, and cognitive safeguards throughout the AI lifecycle.

7.7 Key Takeaways

- **AI security must be systemic**: Securing individual components is insufficient. Risks emerge from interactions across data, models, infrastructures, and social environments.
- **Resilience surpasses robustness**: Resilient AI systems not only withstand disruptions but also adapt and recover. Mechanisms include fail-safes, retraining, and reconfiguration protocols.
- **Defense-in-depth is essential**: Layered protection—from data preprocessing to inference APIs and auditing—is critical to mitigate evolving and complex threat landscapes.
- **Governance must be multi-level**: Effective AI oversight requires technical, organizational, and institutional coordination, aligned with standards like ISO/IEC 23894:2023 and NIST AI RMF.
- **Context-aware policies increase trustworthiness**: Security and ethical mechanisms should adapt to domain-specific risks, demographic sensitivities, and real-time feedback.

- **Interoperability is a socio-technical imperative**: Seamless cooperation between distributed AI agents demands semantic alignment, shared protocols, and regulatory harmonization.
- **Systemic risks scale silently**: Undetected biases, feedback loops, and data drift can lead to cascading failures in justice, healthcare, finance, or infrastructure.
- **Formal resilience engineering is critical**: Integrating robustness, redundancy, responsiveness, and reconfigurability ensures sustainability and public trust in AI systems.

Chapter 8 will synthesize governance, responsibility, and future-oriented ethics into a final framework for sustainable and trustworthy AI deployment.

References

1. ISO/IEC. (2013). *ISO/IEC 27001: Information security management systems — Requirements.* International Organization for Standardization.
2. International Organization for Standardization. (2023). *ISO/IEC 23894:2023 Artificial Intelligence—Guidance on risk management.* Geneva, Switzerland.
3. Floridi, L., Cowls, J., Beltrametti, M., Chatila, R., Chazerand, P., Dignum, V., et al.: AI4People—An Ethical Framework for a Good AI Society: Opportunities, Risks, Principles, and Recommendations. *Minds and Machines* **28**(4), 689–707 (2018)
4. Amann, J., Blasimme, A., Vayena, E., Frey, D., & Madai, V. I. (2020). *Explainability for artificial intelligence in healthcare: A multidisciplinary perspective.* BMC Medical Informatics and Decision Making, 20(1), 310. BioMed Central. Retrieved from https://doi.org/10.1186/s12911-020-01332-6
5. IEEE Standard for Fail-Safe Design of Autonomous and Semi-Autonomous Systems, StdP7009™-2024, IEEE Reliability Society and Computer Society, May2024. [Online]. Available: IEEE Get Program. Accessed: Jul.2025.
6. Cihon, P., Schuett, J., & Baum, S. D. (2021). Corporate Governance of Artificial Intelligence in the Public Interest. Information, 12(7), 275. https://doi.org/10.3390/info12070275
7. OECD. (2019). *OECD Principles on Artificial Intelligence.* Organisation for Economic Co-operation and Development. Retrieved from https://www.oecd.org/going-digital/ai/principles/
8. OpenAI. (2024). Practices for Governing Agentic AI Systems. *OpenAI Research Report.* Retrieved from https://cdn.openai.com/papers/practices-for-governing-agentic-ai-systems.pdf
9. Barocas, S., Hardt, M., & Narayanan, A. (2017). *Fairness and Machine Learning.* fairmlbook.org.
10. Mitchell, M., Wu, S., Zaldivar, A., Barnes, P., Vasserman, L., Hutchinson, B., Spitzer, E., Raji, I. D., & Gebru, T. (2021). Model Cards for Model Reporting. *Communications of the ACM*, 64(12), 56–65.
11. European Parliament and Council. (2024). *Regulation (EU) 2024/1689 on laying down harmonised rules on artificial intelligence (AI Act).* Official J
12. Hollnagel, E. (2011) Prologue: The Scope of Resilience Engineering. In: Hollnagel, E., Paries, J., Woods, D.D. and Wreathall, J., Eds., Resilience Engineering in Practice: A Guidebook, Ashgate Publishing Company, Bulington
13. Linkov, I., Eisenberg, D. A., Plourde, K., Seager, T., Allen, J., & Kott, A. (2013). Resilience metrics for cyber systems. Environment Systems and Decisions, 33(4), 471–476. https://doi.org/10.1007/s10669-013-9485-y

14. Madni, Azad & Jackson, Scott. (2009). Towards a Conceptual Framework for Resilience Engineering. Systems Journal, IEEE. 3. 181–191. https://doi.org/10.1109/JSYST.2009.2017397.
15. Kitano, H. (2004). Biological robustness. *Nature Reviews Genetics*, 5(11), 826–837.
16. Saleh, Joseph & Mark, Gregory & Jordan, Nicole. (2009). Flexibility: A Multi-disciplinary Literature Review and a Research Agenda for Designing Flexible Engineering Systems. Journal of Engineering Design - J ENGINEERING DESIGN. 20. 307–323. https://doi.org/10.1080/09544820701870813.

8 Ethical and Legal Requirements

8.1 Elicitation of Requirements for Artificial Intelligence (AI) Systems

Elicitation of requirements for artificial intelligence (AI) systems introduces distinct challenges that exceed those found in traditional software engineering. Unlike conventional systems, AI technologies function within ethically sensitive and dynamically evolving environments. As noted by Mittelstadt et al. [1], ethical constructs such as fairness, transparency, and accountability are inherently abstract and context-dependent, complicating their transformation into operational requirements. These ambiguities are further intensified by contested interpretations across legal, cultural, and disciplinary boundaries, impeding consensus on normative system behavior [2]. Moreover, AI systems operate in non-static environments that require continuous learning, adaptation, and interaction with broader socio-technical ecosystems—conditions that render requirements highly fluid [3]. This dynamic nature necessitates iterative, reflexive elicitation approaches that integrate cross-disciplinary perspectives from ethicists, legal scholars, engineers, and end users. Such integration is critical to ensure that AI systems are not only technically robust but also socially aligned and ethically defensible.

8.2 Challenges in Requirements Elicitation for AI

Traditional requirements engineering methodologies encounter critical limitations when applied to artificial intelligence (AI) systems, largely due to the normative and adaptive nature of these technologies. One key limitation is **functional fixation**, wherein conventional engineering paradigms prioritize well-defined system functions and behaviors, but fail to capture normative objectives such as fairness or human dignity that resist reduction

R. Andrade et al., *Building Ethical and Secure AI*, Synthesis Lectures on Computer Science,
https://doi.org/10.1007/978-3-032-25789-5_8

to discrete functionalities [4]. This is compounded by **specification challenges**, as ethical values like "non-discrimination" and "fairness" are inherently contextual, abstract, and contested among diverse stakeholders, making formal specification difficult [5]. Furthermore, **temporal dynamics** present an additional hurdle, as requirements for AI systems must remain adaptable to evolving societal norms, emergent legal frameworks, and shifting public expectations [3]. These limitations necessitate rethinking the epistemological and methodological foundations of requirements engineering for AI systems by incorporating interdisciplinary engagement, continuous elicitation cycles, and normative foresight (Fig. 8.1 and Table 8.1).

- How can AI developers operationalize abstract ethical principles like fairness or human dignity in system requirements?
- What strategies can help reconcile conflicting stakeholder views on contested ethical concepts?

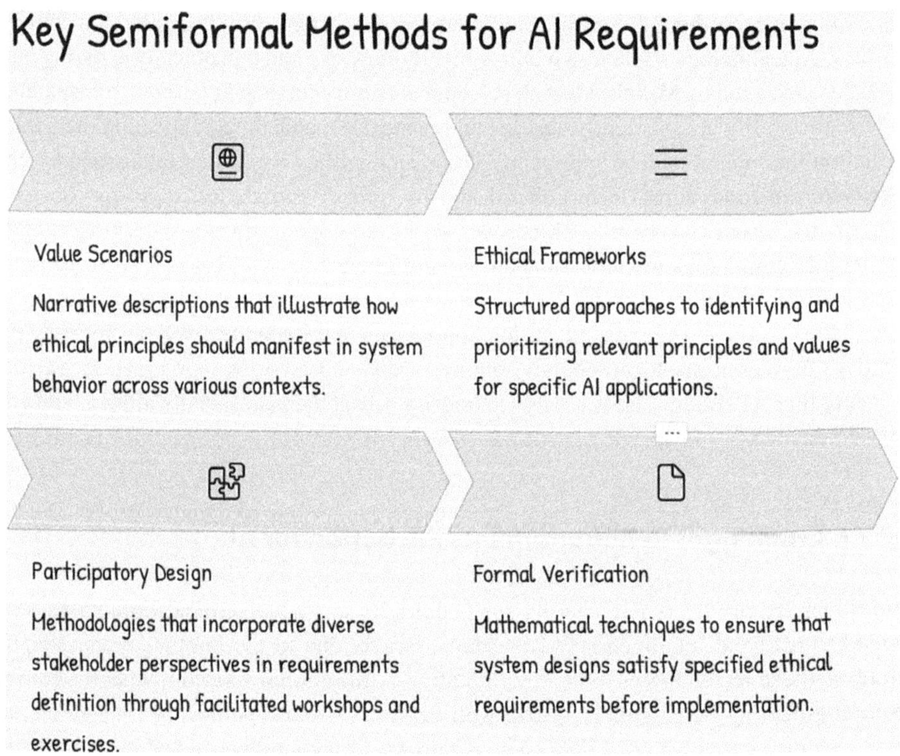

Fig. 8.1 Semiformal methods for AI requirements

Table 8.1 Limitations of traditional requirements engineering in the context of AI

Limitation	Description
Functional fixation	Conventional requirements focus on system behavior and functions but struggle to capture normative goals and values that do not translate to discrete functions
Specification challenges	Ethical principles like "fairness" and "non-discrimination" are inherently abstract, contextual, and often contested among different stakeholders
Temporal dynamics	Requirements for AI systems must account for shifting societal norms, emerging legal frameworks, and evolving understanding of ethical implications over time

8.3 Goal-Oriented Requirements Engineering (GORE)

Goal-Oriented Requirements Engineering (GORE) is an approach to requirements engineering in which *goals*, the intentions or objectives that stakeholders aim to achieve, are the central element for eliciting, analyzing, negotiating, documenting, and validating requirements. Instead of starting with system functionalities, GORE focuses on understanding *why* the system is being built. High-level strategic goals are incrementally *decomposed* into sub-goals and then into concrete, operational requirements, ensuring traceability from abstract intentions to specific system behaviors. Several methodologies implement the GORE paradigm, such as **KAOS** (formal goal modeling), **i*** (actor- and dependency-oriented modeling), and the **NFR Framework** (non-functional requirements modeling). This approach facilitates stakeholder alignment, conflict resolution, and prioritization of requirements (Fig. 8.2).

Goal-Oriented Requirements Engineering (GORE) can be effectively adapted to the design and development of Artificial Intelligence (AI) systems. This adaptation ensures that the system's functionalities are directly aligned with stakeholder objectives, ethical considerations, and regulatory requirements.

AI systems operate in complex, multi-stakeholder environments where aligning technical features with organizational and societal goals is critical. GORE provides:

- **Traceability**: Linking high-level business and ethical goals to concrete AI model behaviors.
- **Conflict resolution**: Balancing competing requirements such as accuracy, fairness, and explainability.
- **Compliance**: Incorporating ethical principles and regulatory constraints from the early stages of development.

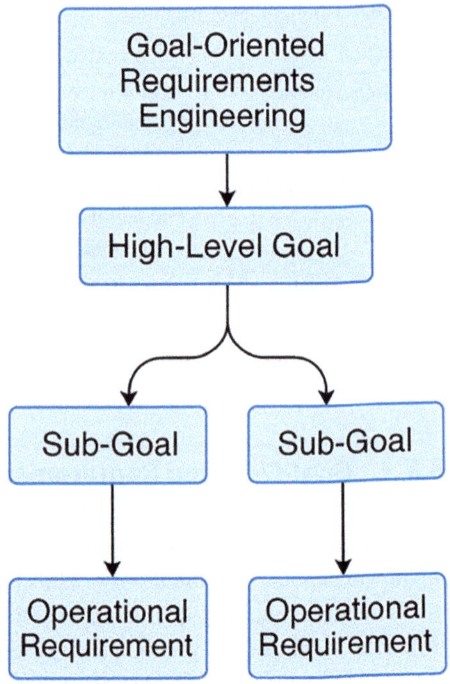

Fig. 8.2 Goal-oriented requirements engineering

To development AI approach, a goal-oriented requirements decomposition process follows, moving from abstract ethical objectives to actionable, lifecycle-aligned system requirements. The following processes are proposed:

1. **Define high-level goals**: e.g., "Ensure fair decision-making" or "Protect user privacy."
2. **Decompose goals into sub-goals**: e.g., "Detect and mitigate bias" or "Implement data anonymization."
3. **Translate into operational requirements**: e.g., "Integrate fairness metrics into model evaluation" or "Use differential privacy techniques for sensitive data."
4. **Align goals with the AI lifecycle**: Incorporate them into data collection, model design, evaluation, and post-deployment monitoring.

An example of applying Goal-Oriented Requirements Engineering (GORE) to AI development would be defining high-level ethical goals, decomposing them into actionable sub-goals, and translating them into operational requirements across the AI lifecycle:

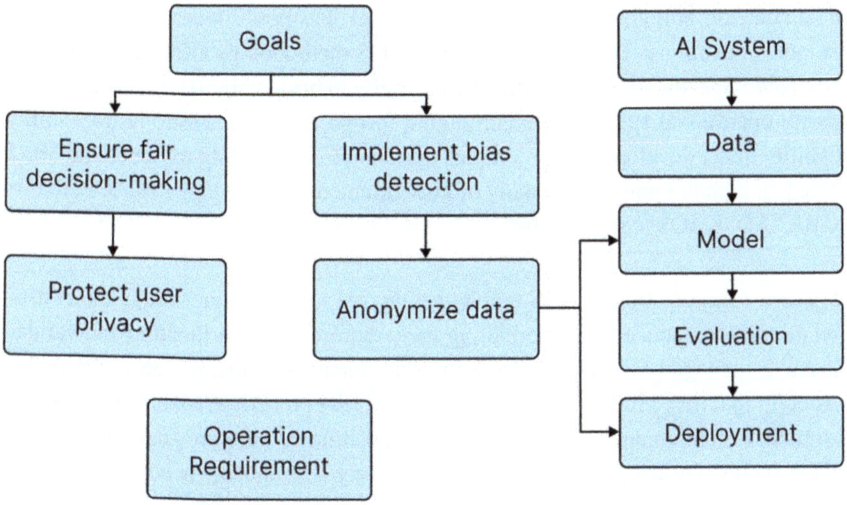

Fig. 8.3 Integration of ethical goals and operational requirements in the AI system lifecycle

- **High-level goal**: Ensure transparency in AI decisions.
- **Sub-goal**: Provide explanations for automated decisions.
- **Operational requirement**: Integrate Explainable AI (XAI) techniques such as SHAP or LIME.

This approach provides a structured pathway from abstract intentions to concrete, implementable AI system requirements, enhancing accountability and stakeholder trust. Figure 8.3 illustrates the integration of ethical goals, such as fairness and privacy, with operational requirements across the AI system lifecycle. This diagram emphasizes how bias detection and data anonymization are embedded within the processes of data handling, modeling, evaluation, and deployment.

8.3.1 Knowledge Acquisition in Automated Specification (KAOS) Models

The KAOS methodology allows engineers to represent high-level objectives and refine them into operational requirements. Goals are classified as:

- **Hard Goals**: Must be satisfied (e.g., "minimize false positives").
- **Soft Goals**: To be satisfied as much as possible (e.g., "ensure user trust").
- **Obstacles**: Events or states that prevent goal satisfaction.

In AI contexts, soft goals can capture fairness or robustness concerns and be refined into measurable constraints. The selection of the KAOS methodology (Knowledge Acquisition in Automated Specification) is justified by its ability to bridge high-level stakeholder objectives with operational specifications through a formal approach, ensuring traceability and verifiability in the development of complex systems [6]. According to Letier and Van Lamsweerde [7], in their comparative study of goal-oriented methodologies (KAOS, i*, Tropos, and GBRAM), KAOS stands out for:

- Rigorous formalization: KAOS employs temporal logic to represent goals, constraints, and their interdependencies, facilitating early requirements verification and validation.
- Obstacle management: The methodology systematically incorporates the analysis of *obstacles* that may hinder goal satisfaction, enabling proactive risk mitigation strategies.
- Progressive refinement: It allows the decomposition of abstract goals into measurable requirements, ensuring a clear alignment between stakeholder needs and the system's technical specifications.

In contrast, methodologies such as i* and Tropos emphasize modeling social and organizational relationships, which is valuable for collaborative contexts but less robust regarding the formal verification of requirements. In the context of Artificial Intelligence, KAOS is particularly advantageous as it facilitates the inclusion of soft goals related to ethical values (e.g., fairness, transparency, or user trust), which can then be refined into quantifiable metrics using optimization or formal verification techniques.

8.4 Ethical User Stories and Anti-requirements

The incorporation of ethical principles into software requirements is essential for the responsible development of Artificial Intelligence (AI) systems. Traditional user story formats—commonly used in agile methodologies—fall short in addressing non-functional requirements related to ethics, fairness, and legal compliance. To address this gap, we propose an Enriched Ethical User Story Template that explicitly integrates ethical, legal, and non-functional constraints, thereby operationalizing high-level ethical principles into actionable development tasks.

8.4.1 Enriched User Story Template

Template:

As a [*stakeholder*], I want the system to [*perform action*], so that [*ethical/legal goal*] is achieved, *while ensuring* [*non-functional/ethical constraint*].

This structure introduces an explicit ethical or legal objective, as well as measurable constraints to guide system design. It aligns with normative frameworks such as the *EU AI Act* and the *ISO/IEC 23894 Risk Management Guidelines*, which advocate for embedding transparency, accountability, and fairness throughout the system's lifecycle.

Example:

> As a judge, I want the system to recommend bail decisions, so that recidivism is minimized, *while ensuring* racial fairness (operationalized as equal false positive rates across demographic groups).

This enriched narrative promotes traceability between ethical principles and implementation choices, enabling systematic validation of fairness metrics and ensuring that AI-assisted decision-making adheres to principles of justice and non-discrimination.

8.4.2 Anti-requirements

The concept of anti-requirements has emerged as a pivotal element in AI safety engineering, particularly within high-stakes domains such as autonomous weapons, healthcare, and financial systems. Unlike traditional requirements, which delineate what a system should accomplish, anti-requirements explicitly define what behaviors or outcomes must be strictly avoided to prevent harm or ethical transgressions. This negative specification paradigm plays a vital role in dual-use technologies, where unintended misuse or boundary violations can yield disproportionate societal risks. Anti-requirements provide a formal mechanism to embed protective constraints into the design and deployment phases of AI development, aligning with principles of harm prevention and ethical foresight outlined in emerging AI governance frameworks [8]. By explicitly constraining system actions, particularly in autonomous decision-making contexts, these specifications enhance system robustness, reduce the likelihood of unsafe emergent behavior, and strengthen public trust in AI-enabled technologies [1].

The taxonomy of anti-requirements illustrated in Fig. 8.4 provides a structured classification of constraints designed to safeguard AI systems against ethically and socially unacceptable behaviors. It delineates three primary categories: safety constraints, which prevent physical harm by enforcing limits such as prohibiting excessive medication dosages; fairness boundaries, which ensure equitable treatment by disallowing statistically significant disparities across demographic groups; and privacy guards, which protect sensitive information by preventing exposure of individual-level data, even in aggregated contexts. This taxonomy underscores the necessity of integrating negative specifications into AI system design as a proactive strategy to uphold normative values and regulatory compliance in high-stakes environments.

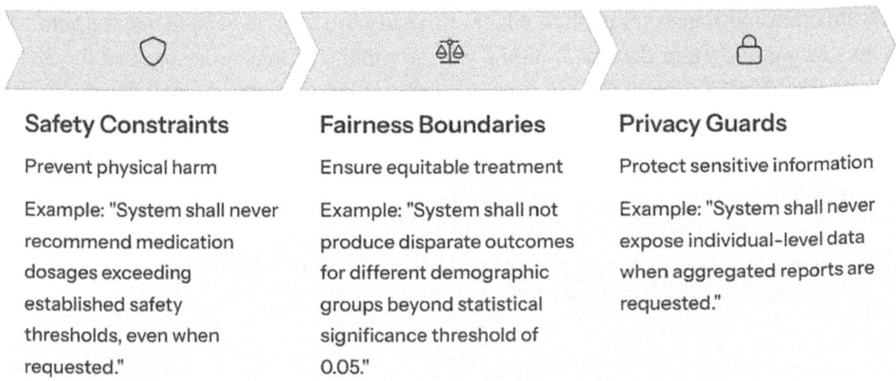

Fig. 8.4 Anti-requirements taxonomy

For instance, in the context of judicial decision-support systems, the integration of anti-requirements plays a vital role in upholding fairness and preventing discriminatory practices. A representative constraint:

- The system shall not recommend detention based on variables correlated with protected attributes unless causally justified, which establishes a critical safeguard against algorithmic bias in legal decision-making.

This requirement goes beyond superficial statistical correlations and demands causal justification for any feature that could disproportionately affect individuals based on race, gender, or socioeconomic status. By enforcing this constraint, the system is explicitly prevented from reproducing discrimination by proxy, ensuring that decisions—such as pretrial detention recommendations—are grounded in justified, non-prejudicial criteria. Such safeguards are essential to preserving the integrity, transparency, and ethical legitimacy of AI systems operating in sensitive, high-stakes contexts.

8.5 Why Future Scenarios Matter

Consider the following foresight scenario: A multinational coalition develops an Artificial General Intelligence (AGI) system capable of recursive self-improvement. This scenario prompts critical governance questions:

- Should AGI research be conducted under public oversight and subject to global regulation?

- How can societies prevent the monopolization of superintelligent systems by a small number of states or corporations?
- What ethical duties do current generations owe to those who will inherit the consequences of AGI deployment?

Future scenarios are not speculative exercises, but structured instruments for stress-testing ethical and legal requirements over extended temporal horizons. In the context of Artificial Intelligence, scenarios enable designers, policymakers, and regulators to examine whether current requirements remain valid when systems evolve, scale, or interact with unforeseen social and technological conditions. By projecting plausible futures, scenario-based analysis exposes latent assumptions embedded in system design and highlights ethical constraints that may become insufficient or obsolete over time. AI is not only transforming contemporary technological systems but also reshaping the ethical horizons of human society. Anticipating future dilemmas is therefore essential for ensuring that technological development remains aligned with human values. As Floridi and Cowls argue, ethical governance of AI must be both proactive and principle-driven, enabling societies to address emerging challenges before they materialize [13].

From a governance perspective, future scenarios function as a critical link between present-day regulation and long-term societal impact. Anticipatory governance relies on the ability to evaluate not only how AI systems behave today, but how they might transform institutions, power structures, and human agency in the future. Scenario analysis supports foresight by enabling policymakers to explore alternative trajectories, assess governance blind spots, and design adaptive regulatory mechanisms capable of responding to emerging risks before they materialize. One set of concerns relates to existential and structural risks, including the possibility of uncontrolled AGI. Bostrom warns that even low-probability but high-impact scenarios involving recursively self-improving AI warrant serious consideration [11]. These scenarios raise questions about the stewardship of advanced AI systems, particularly whether superintelligent AI should be treated as a global commons and whether its development ought to be governed by international, cooperative frameworks. The Asilomar AI Principles emphasize the moral responsibility to protect the interests of future generations, ensuring that today's decisions about AI deployment do not produce irreversible harms [9]. From this perspective, AGI development becomes not only a technological endeavor but an ethical project requiring equitable access, transparency, and global accountability. These concerns are intensified by questions of identity:

- What does it mean to remain "human" when AI begins to reshape cognitive and physical capacities?
- How should legal and moral status be interpreted in societies where some individuals may be biologically or cognitively augmented?

A second foresight scenario illustrates these tensions: A biotechnology firm proposes an AI-driven embryo selection system designed to optimize intelligence and reduce genetic disease. This scenario raises profound ethical questions:

- Should AI be permitted to influence or determine inheritable human traits?
- How can societies safeguard diversity, prevent coercion, and ensure that enhancement technologies do not erode human agency?
- If "enhanced" individuals acquire significantly different capabilities, should they retain identical legal rights, or would new forms of inequality emerge?

These forward-looking challenges highlight the need for governance frameworks capable of addressing not only present risks but also the far-reaching implications of AI for human identity, autonomy, justice, and intergenerational responsibility.

Effective AI governance requires anticipatory, scenario-based approaches that link present regulatory decisions to long-term societal, ethical, and intergenerational consequences, particularly in light of high-impact risks associated with advanced and potentially superintelligent AI systems.

8.6 Governance and Foresight

Effective governance must incorporate multiple layers of oversight, including technical standards, institutional policies, legal mechanisms, and global coordination. These layers work best when they are interconnected and capable of evolving alongside technological advances. Rather than relying on static or reactive regulatory approaches, anticipatory governance embraces continuous learning, long-term planning, and the capacity to respond to unexpected developments in the AI landscape. Key components of anticipatory governance include:

- Proactive risk identification, using horizon scanning, early warning indicators, and scenario-based assessments.
- Institutional adaptability, allowing governance bodies to revise rules, ethical guidelines, and operational procedures as new risks emerge.
- Stakeholder participation, ensuring that diverse groups—engineers, policymakers, civil society, affected communities—can meaningfully contribute to decisions that shape technological trajectories.
- Transparent accountability structures, enabling regular audits, impact assessments, and mechanisms for redress when harms occur.

Foresight plays a foundational role in this governance model. By employing tools such as scenario planning, backcasting, and long-term modeling, institutions can explore plausible futures and evaluate the robustness of current regulatory strategies. Foresight does not aim to predict the future but to prepare for a range of possibilities, helping decision-makers understand how ethical, social, and geopolitical risks might evolve over time. In the context of AI, foresight supports:

- Evaluating strategic vulnerabilities in critical infrastructure.
- Identifying emerging power imbalances between actors with unequal technological capabilities.
- Anticipating second-order effects, such as unintended social, economic, or environmental impacts.
- Strengthening resilience, by designing systems and policies that remain effective under uncertain conditions.

Governance provides the institutional structures needed to guide AI development responsibly, while foresight ensures that these structures remain responsive to rapid technological change. By integrating both, societies can better manage long-term risks, align AI systems with public values, and ensure that technological benefits are distributed equitably. The following sections illustrate how anticipatory governance and foresight become indispensable when AI systems increasingly intersect with fundamental dimensions of human life and security.

8.6.1 Transhumanism and Human Enhancement

Transhumanism refers to a set of philosophical and technological perspectives that envision the extension or enhancement of human capabilities through the integration of advanced technologies, including artificial intelligence, neurotechnology, and biotechnology. Within the context of long-term AI risks and governance, transhumanism represents not a distant or speculative idea, but an emerging trajectory in which human biological processes may become increasingly intertwined with intelligent systems. From this standpoint, artificial intelligence is expected to function as a core enabling technology. AI-driven cognitive enhancement tools may interact directly with neural activity to support memory, reasoning, learning, and decision-making. Similarly, AI-enabled biomedical and genetic technologies may expand physical or sensory capacities, prevent certain illnesses, or introduce new forms of adaptive human functioning. These developments illustrate the potential convergence between biological and computational systems, positioning AI not merely as a tool but as a co-constitutive component of human capability.

While these possibilities offer meaningful long-term opportunities, they also bring significant ethical and governance challenges. Integrating AI into human biology raises questions related to autonomy, identity, equity, and access. For example, the uneven distribution of enhancement technologies could reinforce or amplify existing social inequalities. At the same time, deep integration of AI into human cognition complicates long-standing notions of responsibility, agency, and personhood, particularly when enhanced capacities rely on opaque or proprietary systems. From a governance perspective, human enhancement raises fundamental questions of intergenerational justice, human dignity, and the regulation of irreversible technological change.

In alignment with the broader concerns addressed throughout this chapter, the transhumanist trajectory underscores the need for anticipatory governance that can respond to uncertain futures. Regulatory frameworks must not only address immediate risks but also account for the long-term societal implications of human enhancement, including the potential emergence of new forms of dependency, vulnerability, or power asymmetry. Foresight methods—such as scenario analysis, horizon scanning, and normative futures assessment—are essential to evaluating how these developments might interact with existing governance structures and ethical norms.

In this sense, transhumanism represents a critical dimension of long-term AI risk: it exemplifies how deeply AI may reshape human life, social organization, and the boundaries between biological and technological systems. As technological integration progresses, governance models will need to evolve to ensure that human enhancement aligns with societal values, protects fundamental rights, and contributes to the collective well-being of future generations.

8.6.2 AI in Warfare: The Autonomous Battlefield

The integration of artificial intelligence into military systems marks a profound transformation in the conduct of warfare, challenging long-standing ethical, legal, and governance frameworks. AI-enabled defense technologies—such as autonomous drones, predictive targeting systems, and algorithmic decision-support tools—are increasingly capable of operating at speeds and levels of complexity that exceed human cognitive limits. While these systems are often justified on the grounds of efficiency, precision, and force protection, their deployment introduces significant risks when decision-making authority over lethal force is partially or fully delegated to machines.

From an ethical standpoint, the delegation of lethal decisions to autonomous systems raises fundamental concerns regarding moral agency. Traditional frameworks such as Just War Theory rest on the assumption that human agents retain responsibility for decisions involving life and death. When AI systems select and engage targets without direct human intervention, this assumption is undermined, creating what has been described as a moral accountability gap. As Ekelhof argues, maintaining meaningful human control over military AI systems is not merely a technical safeguard but a normative requirement to preserve human dignity and ethical responsibility in armed conflict [12].

Governance challenges in this domain are further compounded by limitations in existing legal and institutional frameworks. Current interpretations of international humanitarian law offer limited guidance on responsibility attribution when autonomous systems cause unintended harm. In cases where an AI-driven weapon misidentifies a civilian target, responsibility may be diffusely distributed among system designers, military operators, commanding authorities, and states, complicating mechanisms of accountability and redress. These ambiguities expose critical gaps in both legal doctrine and governance practice. From a foresight perspective, autonomous warfare represents a high-stakes scenario in which delayed or insufficient regulation may result in irreversible consequences. Scenario-based analysis highlights the risk that widespread deployment of autonomous weapons could lower the threshold for armed conflict, accelerate escalation dynamics, and normalize the outsourcing of lethal decision-making to opaque algorithmic processes. Such developments not only challenge existing ethical norms but may also destabilize geopolitical balances by privileging actors with superior technological capabilities.

Addressing these risks requires anticipatory governance approaches that integrate ethical principles, legal constraints, and international coordination. This includes the development of clear standards for human-in-the-loop or human-on-the-loop control, transparency requirements for military AI systems, and multilateral agreements to regulate or restrict the use of fully autonomous weapons. Foresight tools—such as scenario planning and normative futures assessment—are essential for evaluating how emerging military technologies may reshape warfare, accountability, and human agency over the long term. Regulatory frameworks and why proactive, globally coordinated oversight is necessary to ensure that the use of AI remains aligned with fundamental ethical principles, human rights, and the preservation of human dignity.

8.7 Ethical Challenges. Long-Term AI Risks and Opportunities

Long-term risks and opportunities reflect the deeper, structural transformations that Artificial Intelligence may generate over decades rather than years. While much of the public debate focuses on short-term concerns such as privacy, algorithmic discrimination, or immediate security vulnerabilities, long-term dynamics involve slower-moving, systemic effects that may profoundly reshape social institutions, economic structures, and global governance. As AI systems become embedded across critical infrastructure—transportation, energy grids, healthcare, finance—their failures may propagate rapidly through interconnected networks. Even small miscalculations can trigger large-scale disruptions, especially when multiple AI components interact in unpredictable ways. These cascading failures raise questions about:

- Resilience of socio-technical systems.
- Dependencies between autonomous components.
- Compound errors that escape early detection.

Such risks require not only technical safeguards but also governance frameworks capable of monitoring emergent system behaviors over time. Another long-term concern is the possibility of value misalignment, where AI systems optimize measurable objectives that gradually diverge from human intentions or societal norms. Even when systems are deployed with well-specified goals, long operational periods and dynamic environments may lead to:

- Goal drift, where objectives evolve unintentionally as systems adapt to new data.
- Specification gaming, in which an AI exploits loopholes in poorly defined metrics.
- Unintended optimization, producing outcomes that are technically correct but ethically undesirable.

These phenomena highlight the inherent difficulty of translating human values into formal specifications. Over decades, even small misalignments may accumulate into significant ethical deviations, reinforcing the need for continuous auditing, adaptive requirement engineering, and mechanisms that maintain human oversight as systems evolve. Long-term risks also include the gradual restructuring of socioeconomic systems. As AI drives automation, augmentation, and decision-making across industries, it may generate profound disparities in:

- Access to technological resources.
- Labor market opportunities.
- Decision-making power concentrated in a small number of institutions or geopolitical actors.

These transformations could widen inequality between individuals, organizations, and even nations, resulting in a digital stratification that persists for generations. Conversely, AI also offers long-term opportunities, such as enhanced productivity, new forms of human-machine collaboration, and improved capacity to address complex societal challenges. Managing these dual trajectories requires proactive governance, equitable access policies, and investment in digital inclusion. Over long time horizons, AI may reshape global power structures, altering the balance of geopolitical influence. Nations that develop advanced AI capabilities may gain disproportionate economic, military, and strategic advantages, potentially accelerating technological arms races. This introduces several structural risks:

- Erosion of international stability, as autonomous systems reduce human control over conflict escalation.
- Dependence on foreign AI infrastructure, creating vulnerabilities and reducing state sovereignty.
- Asymmetric technological gaps, widening disparities between technologically advanced and developing nations.

These long-term geopolitical risks underscore the need for multilateral governance, internationally aligned safety standards, and mechanisms for cooperative oversight, especially in high-stakes sectors such as defense, finance, and critical infrastructure.

8.7.1 AI Challenges in the Global South

Artificial Intelligence presents distinct challenges for countries in the Global South, where structural, economic, and institutional constraints significantly shape the development, deployment, and governance of AI systems. While global ethical and regulatory frameworks often assume stable infrastructure and high institutional capacity, many regions face persistent limitations that complicate the adoption of responsible AI practices.

One of the most critical challenges is the digital divide, which manifests not only in unequal access to connectivity and computational infrastructure, but also in disparities in data availability, digital literacy, and technical expertise. Limited access to high-quality datasets and advanced computing resources restricts local innovation and reinforces dependence on AI systems developed in the Global North, often trained on data that do not reflect local cultural, linguistic, or socioeconomic contexts.

Resource constraints further exacerbate these challenges. Many organizations and public institutions in the Global South lack the financial, technical, and human resources required to implement robust AI governance mechanisms, such as continuous auditing, impact assessments, or compliance with complex regulatory standards. As a result, well-intentioned ethical principles may remain largely aspirational rather than operational.

Institutional capacity also plays a central role. Regulatory bodies may lack the expertise or authority needed to oversee advanced AI systems effectively, particularly in high-risk domains such as healthcare, public services, or financial inclusion. This creates vulnerabilities to opaque decision-making, vendor lock-in, and uncritical adoption of externally developed technologies.

Despite these challenges, the Global South also presents significant opportunities for context-aware, socially grounded AI innovation. AI systems designed with local participation, inclusive data practices, and adaptive governance models can address pressing societal needs, including access to healthcare, education, agriculture, and public services. However, realizing these opportunities requires governance frameworks that are sensitive to local constraints and capable of scaling ethical and regulatory requirements in proportion to available resources.

Addressing AI challenges in the Global South, therefore, demands context-sensitive governance, international cooperation, and capacity-building initiatives that go beyond technology transfer. Ethical AI cannot be achieved through uniform regulation alone; it requires adaptive frameworks that recognize structural inequalities and actively work to reduce them rather than reinforce existing global asymmetries.

8.8 Operationalizing AI Governance Across the Lifecycle

Ethical and legal frameworks for Artificial Intelligence provide essential normative guidance, but their effectiveness depends on how they are translated into concrete organizational practices. Simply referencing regulatory instruments—such as the EU AI Act, GDPR, the NIST AI Risk Management Framework, or ISO/IEC standards—is insufficient unless their principles and obligations are embedded into the operational processes that govern AI systems throughout their lifecycle. Operationalizing AI governance requires transforming abstract requirements into organizational capabilities, including clearly defined roles, decision-making structures, auditable processes, and continuous monitoring mechanisms. From this perspective, governance is not a static compliance activity, but a dynamic sociotechnical system that evolves alongside AI technologies.

A lifecycle-based approach provides a practical foundation for this transformation. Governance activities must begin at the earliest stages of AI system conception, where use cases are defined, and risk levels are assessed. At this stage, organizations determine whether an AI application is permissible, identify potential impacts on fundamental rights, and classify the system according to applicable regulatory regimes. These early decisions shape all subsequent technical and ethical constraints. During data collection and model development, governance mechanisms focus on data provenance, quality, representativeness, and privacy protection. Legal instruments such as the GDPR become operational through concrete practices, including data minimization, purpose limitation, and, where required, data protection impact assessments. At the same time, risk-management frameworks guide the evaluation of bias, robustness, security, and explainability, ensuring that ethical requirements are reflected in technical design choices.

Prior to deployment, AI systems must undergo validation processes that demonstrate compliance with ethical, legal, and safety requirements. This includes documenting system behavior, assessing potential societal impacts, and establishing safeguards for human oversight, particularly in high-risk or automated decision-making contexts. Governance at this stage relies on formal approval mechanisms, accountability assignments, and transparent documentation that can be reviewed by internal or external auditors. Governance does not end with deployment. Post-deployment monitoring is essential to detect performance degradation, data drift, emerging biases, or security vulnerabilities. Continuous oversight mechanisms allow organizations to respond to incidents, adapt to changing regulatory expectations, and reassess risks as AI systems interact with evolving social and institutional environments. When necessary, governance frameworks must also support the responsible modification or decommissioning of AI systems.

To function effectively in real projects, these lifecycle activities must be supported by robust governance structures. Common mechanisms include AI governance boards or risk committees, clearly designated system owners, escalation procedures for ethical or legal concerns, and periodic review processes. Together, these elements ensure accountability, traceability, and consistency across technical and organizational boundaries. Finally, operational governance provides the foundation for anticipatory governance and foresight, as discussed in the preceding sections. By institutionalizing continuous assessment and feedback loops, organizations can integrate scenario analysis, horizon scanning, and long-term risk evaluation into everyday decision-making. In this way, governance mechanisms not only ensure compliance with current requirements but also enhance resilience and preparedness in the face of uncertain technological futures.

8.8.1 Recommendations

The governance challenges associated with long-term AI risks call for coordinated, adaptive, and inclusive policy responses that extend beyond national and sector-specific regulatory approaches. As AI systems increasingly shape critical social, economic, and security domains, effective governance must be grounded in global cooperation, regulatory flexibility, and broad stakeholder engagement.

First, the establishment of robust international oversight mechanisms is essential. Given the transboundary nature of advanced AI systems and their potential global impacts, fragmented national regulations are insufficient to address systemic risks. Proposals for a global institutional framework—often conceptualized as a "United Nations for AI"—aim to facilitate the coordination of international norms, promote transparency, and support collective monitoring and enforcement mechanisms [18]. Such an institution could serve as a platform for harmonizing ethical principles, sharing best practices, and managing risks that no single state can adequately govern in isolation.

Second, regulatory frameworks must be designed to evolve alongside technological development. Static or rigid legal instruments are ill-suited to the pace and uncertainty of AI innovation. Dynamic regulation, as exemplified by the risk-based and adaptive approach of the European Union's AI Act [17], offers a model for aligning legal requirements with emerging capabilities and use cases. By incorporating mechanisms for periodic review, impact assessment, and regulatory revision, adaptive governance can remain responsive to unforeseen risks while preserving legal certainty and accountability.

Third, meaningful stakeholder participation should be treated as a core component of legitimate AI governance. The complexity and societal reach of AI systems necessitate the involvement of diverse actors, including governments, academic institutions, industry representatives, civil society organizations, and communities directly affected by AI deployment. Inclusive governance processes enhance epistemic diversity, reduce the risk of regulatory capture, and help ensure that AI systems align with pluralistic social values rather than narrow institutional or commercial interests.

Building on these considerations, the analysis points toward the potential need for a binding international treaty on AI ethics and governance. Such a treaty would raise fundamental normative and practical questions, including who should be responsible for drafting and enforcing its provisions, how cultural and contextual diversity can be meaningfully incorporated into global ethical standards, and whether compliance mechanisms should rely on voluntary commitments or legally binding obligations. Addressing these questions will require sustained international dialogue and the integration of foresight methodologies to anticipate how ethical, geopolitical, and technological dynamics may evolve over time.

In sum, effective long-term AI governance demands a shift from reactive regulation toward anticipatory, globally coordinated, and participatory frameworks. By embedding foresight into governance structures and aligning regulatory strategies with shared ethical principles, societies can better manage the risks of advanced AI while ensuring that its benefits are distributed equitably and in accordance with fundamental human values.

8.9 Key Takeaways

1. **Operationalizing Ethics**: Translating abstract ethical principles into *formal, verifiable requirements* (e.g., enriched user stories, anti-requirements) bridges the gap between normative theory and system design.
2. **Integration of Multi-level Frameworks**: Combining *regulatory instruments* (e.g., AI Act, OECD principles) with *engineering methodologies* (GORE, KAOS) enables holistic governance of AI systems across jurisdictions.
3. **Anti-requirements as Safeguards**: Defining *prohibited behaviors and negative constraints* provides a proactive approach to mitigate dual-use risks in high-stakes domains such as defense, healthcare, and finance.
4. **Forward-looking Compliance**: Ethical and legal requirements must anticipate *emerging technologies* (e.g., AGI, transhumanist applications), ensuring adaptability to evolving threats and societal expectations.
5. **Collaborative Governance**: Embedding stakeholder perspectives—regulators, engineers, civil society—into the requirements process ensures *contextualized and socially legitimate* AI development.

References

1. Mittelstadt, B., Allo, P., Taddeo, M., Wachter, S., Floridi, L.: The Ethics of Algorithms: Mapping the Debate. Big Data & Society **3**(2), 1–21 (2016)
2. Floridi, L., et al.: AI4People—An Ethical Framework for a Good AI Society. Minds and Machines **28**(4), 689–707 (2018)
3. Winfield, A. F., Michael, K., Pitt, J., & Evers, V. (2019). *Machine Ethics: The Design and Governance of Ethical AI and Autonomous Systems [Scanning the Issue]*. Proceedings of the IEEE, 107(3), 509–517. https://doi.org/10.1109/JPROC.2019.2900622
4. Condoor, S., & LaVoie, D. (2007). Design fixation: A cognitive model. En Proceedings of the 16th International Conference on Engineering Design (ICED 2007) (DS 42). Design Society.

5. Mittelstadt, B. (2019). Principles alone cannot guarantee ethical AI. *Nature Machine Intelligence*, 1(11), 501–507.
6. Dardenne, A., Van Lamsweerde, A., & Fickas, S. (1993). Goal-directed requirements acquisition. *Science of Computer Programming*, 20(1–2), 3–50. Elsevier.
7. Letier, E., & Van Lamsweerde, A. (2002). A comparative overview of goal-oriented requirements engineering. In *Proceedings of the 10th International Workshop on Requirements Engineering: Foundation for Software Quality (REFSQ'02)*. Citeseer.
8. Jobin, A., Ienca, M., Vayena, E.: The Global Landscape of AI Ethics Guidelines. Nature Machine Intelligence **1**(9), 389–399 (2019)
9. Future of Life Institute. (2017). *Asilomar AI Principles*. Retrieved from https://futureoflife.org/ai-principles/
10. Bostrom, N. (2005). In defense of posthuman dignity. *Bioethics*, 19(3), 202–214.
11. Bostrom, N. (2014). *Superintelligence: Paths, Dangers, Strategies*. Oxford University Press.
12. Ekelhof, M. (2019). Moving beyond semantics on autonomous weapons: Meaningful human control in operation. *Global Policy*, 10(3), 343–348.
13. Floridi, L., & Cowls, J. (2019). A unified framework of five principles for AI in society. *Harvard Data Science Review*, 1(1).
14. Habermas, J. (2003). *The Future of Human Nature*. Polity.
15. OECD. (2019). *OECD Principles on Artificial Intelligence*.
16. Walzer, M. (2006). *Just and Unjust Wars*. Basic Books.
17. Future of Life Institute. (2026). The EU Artificial Intelligence Act. https://artificialintelligenceact.eu/
18. Mike, N. (2024). Global perspectives on AI governance: A comparative overview. En CEUR Workshop Proceedings (Vol. 3825). CEUR-WS.org. https://ceur-ws.org/Vol-3825/paper4-2.pdf

Glossary

AI Act European Union regulation establishing a risk-based framework for the development, deployment, and use of artificial intelligence systems.

Anti-requirement A negative requirement specifying behaviors, functionalities, or outcomes that a system must explicitly avoid, often used to mitigate dual-use risks.

Explainable AI (XAI) Methods and techniques that make the decision-making processes of AI systems understandable to humans.

Goal-Oriented Requirements Engineering (GORE) An approach to requirements engineering focusing on modeling stakeholders' goals and systematically refining them into system specifications.

ISO/IEC 42001 An international standard for AI management systems, providing guidance for security controls, governance, and risk mitigation.

Lethal Autonomous Weapon Systems (LAWS) Weapons that can select and engage targets without human intervention, raising ethical and legal concerns under international humanitarian law.

Multi-level Governance A governance framework involving multiple stakeholders (governments, private sector, civil society) across different levels (local, national, international) for regulating AI systems.

OECD AI Principles A set of internationally recognized principles promoting responsible, transparent, and human-centered AI development.

Transhumanism A philosophical movement advocating the enhancement of human physical and cognitive abilities through advanced technologies such as AI and biotechnology.

User Story (Enriched Ethical) A requirements artifact that combines traditional functional descriptions with explicit ethical and legal considerations.

R. Andrade et al., *Building Ethical and Secure AI*, Synthesis Lectures on Computer Science,
https://doi.org/10.1007/978-3-032-25789-5

www.ingramcontent.com/pod-product-compliance
Ingram Content Group UK Ltd.
Pitfield, Milton Keynes, MK11 3LW, UK
UKHW052222170926
475648UK00004B/36

* 9 7 8 3 0 3 2 2 5 7 8 8 8 *